The Dark Road to Triumph

The Dark Road
to Triumph

PASSION WEEK SERMONS FROM A PARIS PULPIT,
INCLUDING MEDITATIONS ON
THE SEVEN WORDS FROM THE CROSS

by Clayton E. Williams

Foreword by Ralph W. Sockman

THOMAS Y. CROWELL COMPANY
New York · *Established 1834*

Acknowledgment is made to the following for permission to quote copyrighted material:

National Publishing Co., Philadelphia, excerpt from *The God of the Lucky* by S. W. Purvis, 1926.

Abingdon Press, Nashville, Tennessee, excerpt from *The Transforming Friendship* by Leslie D. Weatherhead, 1931.

Thornton N. Wilder, excerpts from *Our Town,* copyright 1938 by Thornton N. Wilder.

✤ ✤ ✤ *Foreword*

IT IS HIGH TIME that the reading public should have the benefit of a book by Clayton Williams. Many of his individual sermons have properly appeared in various collections of *Best Sermons*. But now for the first time we have a full-bodied volume from his pen.

This is more than a mere collection of sermons. These are messages centered around one theme and that theme is the center of our Christian Gospel—the Passion and Triumph of Our Lord. It is characteristic of the author that his first book should be based on Christianity's most fundamental tenets, for Clayton Williams never preaches on trivial themes, as I have observed through the years.

His ministry at the American Church in Paris for over a quarter of a century has provided him with an almost unequalled perspective on our contemporary world scene, and his ability has made his pulpit a conspicuous platform for interpreting world issues. His contacts with governmental leaders, his first-hand experiences with American youth amid the personal problems of Paris, his pastorate of a large and changing parish, his services to France which have won for him some of that nation's highest decorations—all these furnish rich background for his messages.

Yet he has kept all these in the background as he focuses the reader's gaze on the heart of our Gospel. Like St. Paul at Corinth, he is determined to deliver one message—"Jesus Christ and him Crucified." And like the Apostle his purpose is to help us "comprehend with all saints what is the breadth and length and depth and height of the love which passeth knowledge."

I have read uncounted books on Our Lord's last days and last words, but this volume has revealed to me new dimensions of Christ's love and passion. As Williams says, many persons have been crucified but it was Christ's character, message, and unique relationship to God which give Good Friday and Easter morning eternal and universal significance. Through these pages we see God on the cross.

Yet reassuring as is his treatment of the deity of Jesus Christ, even more arresting is the author's portrayal of the humanity of Christ. We see Our Lord as no pawn moved across history's board by the Divine Player. Nor is Jesus pictured as so omniscient that he could see clearly the eventual outcome in the midst of his suffering. As Williams says, "His was too great a destiny for his humanity to comprehend." Truly Jesus was "tempted in all points even as we are"—and these points included the temptations to dread pain, to experience doubt, and even at one point, to plumb the depths of despair. All this does not detract from the divinity of Christ, but it does exalt his courage and love.

Ministers will find in these messages fresh material for sermons on the Seven Last Words. I know of no other book in this field which quite so effectively combines poignant feeling with penetrating thought.

And the conclusion strengthens confidence. Speaking of Jesus' last word on the cross, the author says, "Once having submitted oneself to the Father's will, one must commit oneself to the Father's hands." Jesus did. And the final chapters on Easter and its aftermath make us feel that the Heavenly Father's hand did not fail Jesus. Nor will it fail those who follow him.

Ralph W. Sockman

✛ ✛ ✛ Author's Preface

THE VARIOUS CHAPTERS of this book are sermons preached from the pulpit without thought of eventual publication. They are presented essentially as they were delivered.

The writer may seem to be presenting conflicting views and contradictory conclusions. For this he makes no apology. He contends that our knowledge of truth is insufficient to allow us to force it into a fixed consistent system. Truth is greater than any system and validity must be allowed to whole facets of it even though they cannot be fitted into any system. The danger of package-lot truth is that by its very nature it leaves out more than it puts in.

A word should be said about the background of thought behind the meditations on the Seven Words from the Cross. These studies represent the author's attempt to present the crucifixion experience of Jesus, not in terms of those who looked back upon it and drew from it certain theological conclusions, valid though they may be, but rather in terms of the experience of Jesus' own reactions as a man during the last hours of his earthly life.

It seems to the writer that Jesus was the man-God who did not and could not, because of his complete humanity, fully realize that he was God even though he was. He was one with the Father in his thought and action and totally responsive and obedient to the Father but incapable of knowing his Godhead. If he had been capable of this he would not have been man. His role seems to have been that of total obedience and total oneness of spirit but without total knowledge. He was, if you will, God emptied of his Godhead and truly in man's situation and therefore truly beset with man's doubt and temptation to sin, yet not its victim in this respect. That is to say he was in man's situation but not bound by it. He was the victim of sin, but not obedient to it but rather obedient to God.

He was God risking temptation as a man—totally in man's situation and as a man capable of falling a prey to sin and doubt and fear and yet, because of his relationship to God, able to keep free of them. Neither his manhood nor his Godhead was static and fixed but rather dynamic and existential.

Thus the cross was a real crisis for him and not an artificial experience which a self-conscious God endured for metaphysical reasons. In his human situation he actually risked refusal and failure, and it is the writer's feeling that in interpreting the historic event of the cross all attempts to impose deity on Jesus are false and unreal. The experience of the cross must first be viewed in its existential human reality, not with a priori theological premises. Having so seen it one can draw one's theological conclusions.

True, Jesus seems to have had a deep sense of his messianic calling and to have felt that he must be loyal to it. But the very fact that he felt he had been chosen for a special mission and bore a special relationship to mankind must have led to a fearful thought—that throughout the ordeal ahead his calling required that he remain the unbroken incarnation of love, even though he knew that he would be put under extreme pressure to give way. Despite his dependence upon the Father he must have feared lest his humanity could not stand the spiritual test of the cross.

Moreover his profound sense of mission was in itself a danger. We all know what a messianic complex can do, how it can produce a Napoleon or a Hitler once one is convinced of one's role. Unless that sense of mission is tempered, rather than fed, by faith in God and is humble in its dependence upon God, it can be disastrous. All of this must have complicated Jesus' experience.

His very humanity demanded that he live by faith and not by certainty, except the certainty that faith gives. He had to live by faith, but faith is never absolute and his faith was being pushed to the limit at the crucial point. The question was, would it be the breaking point? So far as Jesus was concerned his humanity and his deity were always subject to the possibility of rupture. God could fail in Jesus. That was the risk He accepted in assuming the complete fulness of humanity. Humanity must live by faith and when it is put under strain, can be subjected to doubt and temptation, and fail.

This made the experience of the cross a crucial experience fraught with spiritual risk that endangered both Jesus and his mission. To deny this is to deny his humanity.

It is in this framework of thought that the author has tried to present the crucifixion experience as reflected in the Seven Words from the Cross. He does not pretend that this is the only valid interpretation but contends that it is one which demands consideration and that it actually enhances the stature of Jesus.

C. E. W., Paris, France

✤ ✤ ✤ *Acknowledgments*

N<small>O DOUBT</small> in the course of his reading the writer has picked up ideas and phrases which have fastened themselves in his memory and whose sources are forgotten and must remain anonymous. He is grateful for them but regrets that he can no longer recognize them or acknowledge them.

However acknowledgment is gratefully made for specific excerpts on the copyright page.

I should like to thank the members of my congregation of the American Church in Paris for providing an attentive audience for these sermons and so helping to create them. Thoreau once said that it takes two to speak the truth: one to listen and one to speak. I also owe a debt of gratitude to the Pro-Cathedral Church of the Holy Trinity in Paris, for whose Good Friday Union Services the meditations on the Words from the Cross were prepared and delivered over seven successive years. And I wish to thank the Rev. Morris W. MacFarlane and Miss Gertrude Abrahams for help in preparing the manuscript for publication; Dr. G. Paul Butler for urging that I present this material in book form; and especially Dr. Ralph W. Sockman of Christ Church (Methodist), New York City, for graciously consenting to write the Foreword.

The quotations in the sermons are either my personal paraphrases or my translations.

✢ ✢ ✢ Contents

✤ ✤ ✤ *Palm Sunday*

PALM SUNDAY ENTHUSIASM

And a very great multitude spread their garments in the way; others cut down branches from the trees, and strawed them in the way. And the multitudes that went before, and that followed, cried, saying, "Hosanna to the son of David: Blessed is He that cometh in the name of the Lord!"

And some of the Pharisees . . . said unto Him, "Master, rebuke Thy disciples." And He answered and said unto them, "I tell you that, if these shall hold their peace, the stones would immediately cry out."   Matt. 21:8, 9; Luke 19:39, 40

THE PALM SUNDAY NARRATIVE has always been popular. Through the centuries it has taken a hold upon men's imaginations, partly because of its contrast with the tragic days that came later, but more particularly because a celebration always attracts people.

One can get a crowd out for a ceremony almost any time, especially if it is colorful, and a procession is still more appealing. People come out hours in advance for a coronation procession. Some even take their places on the curb the night before. A holiday and a parade will always bring a crowd.

In this case the celebration and the procession combined to make the first Palm Sunday an outstanding occasion. This was Passover week and the capital was crowded with pilgrims who transformed its narrow streets into a hive of humanity. That in itself was enough to turn even the simplest group of marchers into a triumphal procession once it got under way and caught the attention of the populace.

Many processions had been seen by the people of Jerusalem in its day. As Dr. S. W. Purvis in *The God of the Lucky* says: "They were connoisseurs in triumphal parades. Solomon's inaugural, the colorful visit of the Queen of Sheba, and the return of Jewish military heroes from their successful wars, which called forth such hymns as the Twenty-fourth Psalm, were all traditions that stirred imaginations. No doubt there were some still living who could remember how Herod the Great had come riding into the city at the head of an army to defy the haughty Sanhedrin that had summoned him to trial. Perhaps some had seen Cassius, the gray-headed triumvir, arriving with his Roman cohorts. And some had seen the swift-moving Parthians come sweeping victoriously over Palestine to seat Antigonus on the throne. And there were many who had seen Herod, backed by the might and glory of Rome, leading Mariamne, his bride, as he entered the City of David to seat himself in splendor on the blood-stained throne in the ancient capital of Judea."

But today another king was entering Jerusalem. True, there was no tramp of feet marching in measured cadence, no disciplined ranks, no glittering helmets or array of banners, no rows of Roman short-swords or long Thracian pikes, and no colorful war horses or battle chariots; no martial music, no mounted trumpeters to herald his coming. But it was a royal entry, none the less.

There is little doubt but that the triumphal entry had been carefully planned by Jesus to fit the details of the prophecy of Zechariah, and thus to form a deliberate, dramatic declaration of his challenge to his people. Despite the fact that it proclaimed him a Prince of Peace, it was enough to fire the imaginations of the passionate band of patriotic pilgrims who accompanied him. Hopes had run high and there was undoubtedly a tendency to look upon him as the long awaited emancipator.

Enthusiasm is contagious, and within a short time hymns and shouts passed from mouth to mouth, and religious fervor and patriotic zeal took hold of the crowd. Running on ahead they threw down their cloaks and stripped branches from the palm and olive trees and spread them before him, crying, "Hosanna!"—which is to say, "Now save us!"—"Blessed is the King that cometh in the name of the Lord."

There is a naive sincerity and spontaneity about such devotion that is attractive. After all, what did Jesus think of all this? There must have been many things about it that were distasteful to him. Ordinarily Jesus avoided crowds and the spectacular. If there was to be a transfiguration he reserved it for the intimate few. Again and again the multitude sought him only to find that he had gone from them. His miracles drew great crowds but they were a constant source of embarrassment. Once he had had an unfortunate experience with a crowd when he fed the five thousand and found that they were more interested in his power to provide bread than in his message to their hearts. The Master distrusted crowds, but no doubt they often presented a subtle temptation; he realized how easily he could meet the popular demand and swing the multitude to his banner, if he wished.

Today he cherished no illusions about either the source or the extent of the crowd's enthusiasm. He knew it was misguided and short-lived. Ordinarily he unmasked superficial expressions of loyalty, exposing the rootless allegiance of shallow spirits, insisting that men count the cost. Jesus made the way hard, for knowing men's hearts as no other did, he knew the effervescence of shallow enthusiasm. Superficial enthusiasm is almost always born of a lack of understanding of a situation. It must have meant much anguish of heart to Jesus to realize how little they understood his kingship.

There is no question but that he was misunderstood. The enthusiasm of the people was born in large part of a misconception of his intention, perhaps even of a willingness to let their hopes distort the facts. But being misunderstood was not a new experience for Jesus. Even those nearest to him misunderstood him, and he spent much of his time trying to make his message clear to the sluggard minds of his hearers who failed to understand him, not because they were dull witted, but because they were obsessed with their own ideas and desires. They always read their hopes into everything he said.

When Jesus spoke of victory, they thought of victory in battle; he thought of triumphant living—"To him that overcometh will I give the crown of life."

When Jesus spoke of liberty, they thought of political liberty, escape from the yoke of Rome; he thought of inner freedom of spirit—"Ye shall know the truth and the truth shall make you free."

When Jesus spoke of strength and power, they thought of armed forces and physical might; he thought of the strength of courage and faith—"Ye shall receive power after that the Holy Ghost is come upon you."

When Jesus spoke of enlarged borders and a greater destiny, they thought of conquest and more territory; he thought of broader sympathies and broken barriers of class and race—in him "there is neither Greek nor Jew . . . Barbarian, Scythian, bond nor free."

When Jesus spoke of treasures, they thought of possessions; he thought of the riches of the heart.

When Jesus spoke of a more abundant life, they thought of a change of circumstances; he thought of more vitality of spirit—"A man's life consisteth not in the abundance of the things which he possesseth."

Thus they misconstrued his purpose and tried to squeeze his great conceptions into the narrow pigeonholes of their little minds, just as we do. Yet they were sincere in their enthusiasm, even though they saw a throne where he saw a cross—"Be it far from thee, Lord."

Another day Jesus might have dealt summarily with such impetuous fervor, but not today! He had faced and accepted the cross. There was no more danger in the crowd's acclaim.

Moreover he not only permitted it, he seemed to feel it was necessary. Here for a moment we get an insight into his infinite patience and his all-embracing compassion for us.

Jesus recognized the joy, the expectancy, the devotion of the multitude, and he did a gracious and beautiful thing. Despite the fact that he knew that they misunderstood him, that they had no true idea of what his kingship meant, and despite the fact that he knew that they would let him be crucified before the week was over, Jesus graciously accepted their enthusiastic acclaim without a sign of cynicism. It is as though he wanted to give the people one fine, high moment on which to look back. The loyalty of these simple Galileans was so genuine!

He saw it all for what it was, and took it for what it presumed to be. When they cried, "Hail to the King," they were saying more than they knew. He *was* the king—the king of men's hearts.

To be sure, the crowd did not understand the significance of that title, but neither do we! To be sure, they did not comprehend the meaning of his coming, but neither do we!

It was as though Jesus wanted the people to have a beautiful memory of a day when they had given all their enthusiasm to admiration and hope. What if it did all come to nought? Are our best dreams and hopes futile because they are but faint fragments of what they should be?

He wanted them to have this one opportunity to give full reign to their hearts' devotion, that they might look back and say, "I was there. I remember well the exultation of that moment. True, it all came to nothing, but it was good to have done it. I should do it again, for he was a Prince of Men. True, we were blind. We should have understood. We might have saved him. But at least I gave him my loyalty for a day!"

It is true that danger lurks here. As someone has said, "It is easy simply to sing lovely hymns with our lips and not lift the voices of our lives in praise." It is easy to honor his entry into Jerusalem but to refuse him entry into our lives, easy to call him, "Lord! Lord!" but to deny him lordship in our hearts. Enthusiasm is in danger of that.

It was not adequate, this fanfare of "Hosannas" and palm branches. Jesus knew that, but he accepted the enthusiasm of these Galilean pilgrim-followers as the earnest of something not yet attained, something that they followed in the dimness of their hearts. And he rejoiced in it.

That was typical of Jesus' compassion. He made a fine distinction between idle sentimentality and true sentiment. Merciless with sham and superficiality, he was infinitely tender and responsive to an act of true devotion. It was a very precious thing.

There is no finer picture in the whole story of the life of Jesus than that of the nameless woman who broke in on the formal dinner party in the home of Simon of Bethany, and out of the depth of her love and gratitude, poured the contents of a costly alabaster urn of precious perfume upon Jesus' head. It meant so much to the Master that he responded at once and said, "Wherever the Gospel is preached, what she has done will be told in memory of her." That's how much he thought of devotion!

But tight-minded, economical Judas, secure and calculating in his efficiency, even in his charity, thought it should have been sold and given to the poor. This drew the Master's indignation, and he cried out in protest, "But Judas, devotion has no price; you cannot buy or sell it. It is priceless. With such devotion in your heart, you will always be able to take care of the poor, and every other need in life."

It is no wonder that when the circumspect and respectable Pharisees, shocked at this effervescent expression of emotion on the part of the Galilean pilgrims, suggested that Jesus quench their enthusiasm and quiet them down, the Master turned to their spokesman and cried, "Man, I tell you that if these should hold their peace, the very stones would cry out." He knew that it was folly to suppress enthusiasm when it might be used.

There are some who look with dismay upon our emotion, insisting that we are rational beings moved by logic; but, thank God, we can feel with our hearts as well as think with our heads. We live in a world of values, not arguments, and all the finest things of life are the things of the heart—art, music, literature, and poetry; a mother's love, a father's courage, and a patriot's devotion. Power flows from enthusiasm. Nothing of any importance has ever been done without it, and the movement or organization that can capitalize on that enthusiasm and turn it into enduring loyalty will be the movement that will accomplish things and survive.

Enthusiasm, of course, can be misappropriated by a Hitler or a Napoleon or a Mussolini, but that does not invalidate it. Quite the contrary! Jesus admired honest enthusiasm even in forthright sinners. It was the righteous repressions of the Pharisees that made them "impossible saints."

The problem of enthusiasm is not a problem of suppression, but of direction and deepening. Jesus did not repudiate their enthusiasm; he led it on to deepen into true loyalty in the presence of the Cross. That is the solution for Palm Sunday enthusiasm. Mistaken though it may be, it can be transformed into a deeper lasting loyalty when it has faced the Cross. Palm Sunday must face Good Friday.

And mistaken though it may be, he accepts our devotion if it is sincere even though we too have no adequate conception of what it really means to be his disciples. He knows how often our hopes outrun our persistence, how often our enthusiasm lags and faints. But he is willing to take the loyalty of our hearts and lead it into a larger understanding of his purposes if only we will follow him and give him what devotion we can. For enthusiasm and admiration can be transformed by his grace into loyal discipleship at the foot of the Cross.

THE CHALLENGE OF PALM SUNDAY

And when he was come into Jerusalem, all the city was moved, saying, "Who is this?"   Matt. 21:10

IF YOU WILL LOOK at the last week of Jesus' life you will note that it was a week of challenges initiated very specifically by the triumphal entry of Palm Sunday, which the Master had planned to fit all the imagery associated in the minds of the people with the fulfillment of the well-known prophecy of Zechariah. The triumphal entry was not a mere incident but a deliberate, dramatic declaration of what he stood for, calculated to challenge their attention and to stir their imaginations and arouse their consciences and to give his people one last opportunity to understand the issue involved in his coming.

And from that time on, by word and act, Jesus kept his challenge before both the people and the authorities until it issued in the final challenge of the cross. We may think of Jesus as the gentle teacher expounding his philosophy of love on the peaceful mountainside or by the quiet lake shore with the calm assurance of one who presents the eternal verities. But this last week presents quite another picture, the picture of a bold, determined, outspoken figure striking at the heart of pride and iniquity in all of its forms, no less poised, no less compassionate, no less magnanimous, but strong, resolute, courageous, incisive, and challenging, drawing the issue clearly and sharply in unceasing conflict with the existent order.

It is little wonder that this audacious declaration in the triumphal entry, clothed in the pageantry that his followers gave it, aroused questions in the minds of the people. One after another—the Roman guard surprised by this demonstration on the part of the pilgrims, the Jerusalem townsfolk who hearing the noise of singing and the shouts of the throng peered out of their windows, the austere authorities troubled by the enthusiasm of the crowd, and the young idealists attracted and inspired by the ardor of the pilgrims —all asked the same question, "Who could this be? Who is this?"

To each of them Jesus' coming was a challenge and each responded differently, according to his background, his outlook, his hopes and his desires. The vital importance of the ordinary trend of a man's life lies in the direction in which it leads him and the reactions which it makes inevitable. So the response of each group to the challenge of Jesus was determined both by their capacity to see and by the aspirations that lay nearest their hearts.

Some, actuated by their fervent patriotism and their hope for national freedom, saw in him a political leader and a potential deliverer, and they met him with the acclaim due to a king.

Some who wanted nothing better than to be left alone to pursue their own interests and to follow their own ways saw in him only the leader of a colorful procession, the object of a popular demonstration that for the moment was disturbing their peace, and as tolerant men they met him with curiosity and indifference.

Some who were entrenched in privilege, reaping benefit from the exploitation of vested interests, like the chief priests and authorities, saw in him a threat to their privileges, and they met him with open animosity.

Some who were charmed by his graciousness, intrigued by his astuteness, and astonished by his boldness, saw in him their ideal, and they met him with unfeigned admiration.

And some who were deeply moved by the truth of his Word, strengthened by the contagion of his faith, redeemed by the power of his gracious compassion, saw in him a message from God—a vision of God's intention for man and the earnest of a new life and a new Kingdom of the spirit —and they met him with grateful devotion and loyal discipleship.

Every man saw him and responded to him according to the hopes he cherished and the interests he lived by. And it is so today. The world has not changed, nor have men's hearts, and these different reactions are typical of the world's reaction to Christ today. We use him, we admire him, we ignore him, we resist him or we follow him, and exploitation, adoration, indifference, antagonism, or consecration still determine, as in Jesus' own day, the response of men's hearts to the Master of the world.

There are, for example, some of us who see him as the protagonist of our own desires and outlook, who use Jesus for our own purposes, much as the patriots of Jesus' day acclaimed him for the fulfillment of their own selfish hopes and ambitions. We see very much what we want to see, and we tend to interpret life in terms of what we most desire. Religion is ever being prostituted to become the tool of man's desires, and even Jesus has been twisted and distorted to accommodate nearly every project that has actuated the human heart. He has been made the protector of vested interests and of divine rights, the instigator of revolutions and the supporter of wars, the father of nearly every form of political theory—capitalism, socialism and communism—the conservator of both outworn and false sciences. Conflicting patriotisms have invoked his name and warring nations have sought victory through his power. Even the Church and religious groups have presented Christ as a talisman, a magic name to bring happiness. That is the tragedy of confusion that always happens when men seek to use Christ rather than be used by him.

Are we using Christ for our own purposes?

Again there are some of us who think of Jesus as the great ideal, the supreme object of our admiration, but one whose teachings and spirit are so far removed from the realm of ordinary life as to be absolutely impracticable. We can think of nothing more beautiful than the Sermon on the Mount, and nothing more unsuited to practical living.

That was one of the things that Jesus feared. He was not afraid of opposition and he was not even afraid of the

cross in the end. But when on the Mount of Transfiguration
Peter suggested that they build tabernacles there, Jesus
withdrew and told them that it was time that they returned
to their mission among the people. He looked about him and
saw that the spiritual leaders of the day were avoiding the
imperative of the prophets by whitening their tombs and
worshiping their memory; he saw the power for frustration
that superficial worship held.

And we still fall athwart that tendency today. It is so
much easier to give our approval to Christ than to give our
obedience. As someone has said, the Church is full of
persons who would be equally shocked to find Jesus' deity
denied or his teaching applied. Admiration, valuable as it
is, is futile until it issues in consecrated living.

Are we giving Christ our admiration or obedience?

Again, there are some of us whose consciences have
been pricked who see all too clearly the fundamental issue
between Jesus' teaching and spirit and the existent order of
things in our lives and our society; and consequently we fear
and resist him. He is the troubler of our peace. He has set up
a conflict within our hearts that has aroused all the forces
of resistance within us and we know him as the "Hound of
Heaven" and would do almost anything to do away with him,
to be left to our own devices, to enjoy our own indulgences.

When Jesus rode into Jerusalem the leaders ignored
him until he went into the temple and upset things there.
But when he invaded the temple of their pride, their prejudices, and their privilege, they cried out, "Crucify him!" And
so it is with us, only we take it out on someone else near
at hand.

Let religion be a matter of sweet sentiments, and no
one cares. But let it interfere with our affairs and demand
forgiveness and justice and the resolution of our prejudices
and the sacrifice of our privileges, and we are all aroused.

Christ can touch anything but our practices. To paraphrase Halford Luccock's comment, Jesus was not crucified for saying, "Consider the lilies how they grow," but for saying, "Consider the life of this people, how corrupt it is." But thank God, out of the tensions of this inner conflict there can come, by his grace, peace and life.

Are we afraid to let Christ challenge certain areas of our life?

Then there is another group, not large perhaps but very vital, who have renounced their own inadequate past and have turned to him as Lord of their lives and have become, timidly perhaps but none the less truly, his devoted followers, not ready yet to face a cross but struggling along in his steps, seeking his Kingdom.

Is he too the Master of our lives?

These then were the groups that heard his challenge and responded. But there was another group, so little aware of him and of all he stood for that they hardly knew that he had passed until he was gone. There are those who are so immersed in their own designs, so absorbed in their own concerns, in enjoying life or pursuing it, that Christ simply is not a factor of any importance. He does not count one way or the other. He is ignored.

There is a profound tragedy in the ignored Christ that is even greater than that of the crucifixion. We think of Palm Sunday as a day of rejoicing. We think of the triumphal entry and we see the throng of ardent pilgrims, their faces lighted with hope, their hearts aglow with eagerness, and we hear the impassioned cries of "Hosanna" and "Halleluia," and the swelling chorus of Psalms; and we think of it as a day of glorious triumph.

But that was not all. There was a great city going about its business almost unaware of the Master's presence. Oh, to be sure, the noise and clamor piqued their curiosity for a moment and the merchants looked out from their stalls and the housewives paused in their housework to come to the doorway and a few of the aristocrats peered out through latticed windows in sheer wonderment. But when all they saw was a Galilean peasant on a donkey and a crowd of pilgrims in up-country smocks, no one cared for long what it was. The merchants turned again to the arrangement of their stocks to catch the eye of the increasing crowd of pilgrims. The women returned to the preparation of their houses for the guests that were sure to come with the feast time. And those behind latticed windows turned to give the final instructions for the procuring of the paschal lamb or the sending of their servants to meet the expected friend.

The tragedy of Palm Sunday was the tragedy of the ignored Christ. He had life to offer them but he could not give it to them. The light of the world was among them but they could not see him. They were blind. The celestial message of grace was being spoken to them but they could not hear it. They were deaf. The redeemer-creator spirit was among them but they could not feel it. They were insensitive. There were many who never saw him though he walked their streets. There were many who never heard him though they stood in his presence. As Leslie Weatherhead has said, "The tragedy of the blind man is not that he trips on the curb and meets tragedy from without. It is that he cannot revel in the world of sight. Sunset and star, sunshine and flowers mean nothing to him." Helen Frazee-Bower has well expressed it in a sonnet:

> God pity eyes that have not seen the dawn,
>   Twilight, or shadow, or wind-blown tree,
> But pity more the eyes that look upon
>   All loveliness and yet that cannot see;
>
> God pity ears that have not caught the notes
>   Of wind or wave or violin or bird,

But pity more, that daily music floats
    To ears that hear and yet have never heard.

God pity hearts that have not known the gift
    Of love requited, comfort, and caress,
But, O God, pity more the hearts that drift
    From love's high moment to forgetfulness.

This is the tragedy of common sense:
    To dim all wonder by indifference.

The hero-worship of the triumphal throng may have been mistaken but it represented a sensitivity to spiritual values. Blindness, deafness, and hardness of heart are the great tragedies of life because they mean lost opportunities.

One of the saddest stories is the story of an incident that occurred in the life of the great Viennese surgeon, Dr. Lorenz. When he was in America some years ago there were a great many requests for his aid and he could not possibly meet them all. A woman in one of our big cities where it was expected that Dr. Lorenz would come made efforts to get in touch with him to ask his help in curing her child. Dr. Lorenz was in the habit of taking a daily walk immediately after lunch each day, no matter how threatening the weather, and he instructed his chauffeur to come for him in case of a hard storm. One afternoon it began to rain, gently at first, but after a bit it was evident that a heavy storm was in the offing. As the rain began, the woman who desired the doctor's help went out onto the front porch to look at the sky and to see that the wicker furniture was safely put away. While she stood there an elderly gentleman came up the walk toward the house, his light summer suit almost soaked with the rain. Removing his hat he said in a slightly foreign accent, "Madam, may I sit on your veranda till the rain stops?" Indifferently and without a word the woman motioned him to a chair and though he was elderly and wet she did not ask him to enter but turned on her heel and went into the house, leaving him there on the porch. After a while there was a sudden creaking of brakes as a car drew up and a chauffeur came running frantically up the walk with an umbrella and a raincoat. From within the woman saw the incident but thought little of it until she read in the paper the next morning that the famous surgeon had been marooned in a rainstorm and had taken shelter on a porch where he had suffered nothing more than two chills, one from his damp clothes and the other from the woman of the house. In dismay she rushed to the hotel only to learn that a few moments before, Dr. Lorenz had taken the train for the East, never to return. A lost opportunity!

The Gospel is the Gospel of the eternal opportunity. God's willingness knows no limits but man's willingness can be limited by his spiritual callousness. A man may come to church and be completely bored and yet it may not be the church's fault. He may have lost his capacity to hear the voice of God.

Today in the midst of all the confusion and tension of conflicting forces the hope of the world lies in the spirit of Christ and the resources that are in him. But men can be so absorbed in their own little plans for security or comfort or merely getting on, or a nation so concerned with its own problems, so self-centered as to be completely oblivious to his challenge and to the opportunity that lies in him until, as it was for Israel, it is too late.

And so Jesus' coming to Jerusalem was both a challenge and a judgment, for men are judged by their reaction to Christ and what he stands for. Every opportunity is also a judgment, and that last week was a week of judgments. Judas was judged by a broken urn of ointment and by thirty pieces of silver. Two bits of copper and a temple offering-box judged the blindness of those who failed to see the sincere loyalty of a poor widow woman. Peter was judged by the taunts of a serving maid by the fireside, and a few fluttering doves and bleating lambs and some overturned tables brought judgment to Annas and Caiaphas, the high priests. Pilate thought that he was judging Jesus but he himself was being judged by his own decision and even today the world remembers that judgment against him.

And so it was with everyone who came in contact with Jesus up to the last hour on the cross, and even then the two companions that hung by his side were judged out of their own mouths, and one found mercy. That cross became a judgment seat for everyone who saw it and for all who heard of it—"to the Jews a stumbling block and to the Greeks foolishness."

But are we really greatly different today from these people of Jerusalem? Have we kept our lives sensitive to the word that God would speak to our hearts? Or are we so immersed in the pursuit of prosperity and security and distraction that we have focused our desire upon these things and have become impervious to the word that God seeks to bring to our lives today?

By every possible means, and especially and particularly by that cross, the great Redeemer Spirit of this universe is trying to bring his gracious mercy and love to bear upon our life, to lift it out of its littleness and its folly, out of its frustration into victory, out of its cramping self-centeredness into a deeper and richer life. And all too often we who need him so desperately are so concerned with the things that pass for life which capture our desires and enthrall our energies that we never feel or know his deep cross-centered concern for us. We go our ways blind to his overtures, deaf to his word for us, unconscious of his presence, with all our time and interest and effort absorbed in secondary things, as though life really lay in what we can see and feel and manipulate and manage; and all the time his spirit is trying to break through and touch our lives and save us from the pride and selfishness that is destroying us. But we have never really quieted our hearts to hear him or disciplined our spirits to respond to him or desired him with a great enough desire to know him. And so his word falls upon our ears unheeded and his healing presence is unfelt and we are left to ourselves alone in a universe where really Christ reigns, bereft of his presence because we are too blind to recognize his Lordship and too careless to open our hearts to his spirit.

And so the challenge of Christ goes on, and the judgment, for you and me. For all of us are judged by that cross and by our response to the eternal love that God manifested there and the redemptive power that flows from it.

✦ ✦ ✦ *Maundy Thursday*

BETRAYAL

*The Lord Jesus the same night in which he was be-
trayed took bread: and when he had given thanks,
he brake it, and said, "Take, eat; this is my body,
which is broken for you: this do in remembrance of
me."*   *I Cor. 11:23, 24*

ON THE SAME NIGHT in which he was betrayed! It is a
dastardly thing to be betrayed, to have someone exploit our
good will for their advantage or to vent their spleen, to suffer
the treachery of one in whom we have confidence. It is a
soul-devastating experience. It violates our trust, our sense
of justice, and destroys that mutual confidence which is the
basis for all human relations. It strikes at the very heart of
man's innate faith.

And yet betrayal is one of the persistent problems of
our existence. In one form or another we have all experienced
it, when we have been swindled in some transaction, when
the rare article which we had bought turns out to be a mere
imitation, or the contract we made is violated, or when someone in whom we have put our faith turns against us and is

our undoing. That is one of the fearful experiences which characterize the modern police state. Betrayal by one's neighbors or even by members of one's own family has happened all too often under totalitarian regimes.

Sometimes our own idealism betrays us. Consider the plight of those honest if misguided idealists who helped the Communist forces to come to power in the satellite countries, only to find their ideals betrayed by the very men whom they helped. Or it may be that we are betrayed when the course of events undoes all for which we have worked and on which we have counted. Our popular Western success philosophy to the contrary, one can cite innumerable cases where the fruits of honest effort and genuine goodness have not been success and public respect but failure and shame, cases where those who have done the most for good causes have suffered the greatest opposition and tasted the fruits of bitterness. Life is always suffering betrayal and the tragedy is that we have not found an effective technique with which to meet it; rather most often we fall a prey to indignation and resentment.

At heart what hurts and arouses us is the way in which goodness is constantly being betrayed by the turn of events which often seem to deny all justice and to obliterate any evidence of God's action to conquer or crush evil. It strikes at our faith. I think there is where we come closest to the heart of this whole problem, for the force of all other betrayals is born of that deep sense of injustice which comes to a focus in the crisis of Jesus' own encounter with evil both in his life and on the cross, for if anyone felt the force of betrayal it was Jesus. If there were any justice in events he should have had his efforts crowned with success. And yet it was just because of his loyalty to truth and goodness that he suffered the opposition and persecution which haunted his life. His goodness should have led to triumph but it did not.

It did not culminate in a Kingdom of Heaven on earth, with security and harmony and the destruction of evil in any Twenty-third Psalm sort of way; instead it led to persecution, defeat, and a cross.

To be sure, deep down in his heart he knew that the grain must die to bring forth fruit and he told his disciples as much, but the patent logic of his experience indicated that goodness was not consummated in triumph or success. More often than not his words brought no repentance on the part of his hearers but only indifference, resistance, or antagonism. "He came unto his own, and his own received him not."

In a sense he was betrayed not only by Judas but by life. A life of love and service had led not to popular acclaim and acceptance but to persecution and crucifixion.

Christians too often make the mistake of reasoning that the good life must lead to felicitous circumstances and the successful termination of our good enterprises. Jesus was far too realistic to teach that. He never underestimated evil's power. He knew too well its capacity to impose suffering and twist and thwart life's best efforts. He knew that it was no phantom opposition force, no figment of the mind. He knew that it had power, power which should be feared, power which in his case it finally declared by taking him into its cruel hands and nailing him flat to a cross. The incongruity of it all must have troubled his soul on more than one occasion, as it does ours.

The depth of his understanding of evil's power to destroy life must have given tremendous poignancy to the temptation to doubt God's sovereignty over life. After all, that is the heart of doubt, to look out upon life's devastating evil forces and question God's power to overcome them.

Jesus saw what evil so often did to goodness, how often life's finest efforts were betrayed and life's nascent hopes cut short, how often self-righteousness, pride, and might trampled on simple faith and sincere devotion and tried to crush them. And aware of that power and considering the treatment life had measured out to him, it would not have been surprising if there had been occasions when he wondered if that cross that loomed up on the horizon might not end in final failure for him—if the evil which had pursued his life might not finally grasp him and destroy him.

As his mission continued, the power of the opposition grew, and his work culminated not in a visible Kingdom but in a destructive cross. Certainly that did not look like the vindication of God's power but rather its betrayal, and there must have been moments when it troubled his soul.

Conclusive evidence of the force of that logic may be found in his response to Peter. Peter declared that Jesus, of all men, ought not to have to suffer a cross, and Jesus felt the tempter's presence in Peter's words. The final impact of this temptation seems to have come to a focus as he faced the cross in the hours which preceded the crucifixion. It was then that he suffered the most, not in anticipation of physical pain so much as in the fact that he still felt the impact of the argument that goodness ought to culminate in success and evil be crushed and vanquished, not suffered.

That is what Jesus shrank from in the Garden. When he prayed, "Let this cup pass from me," it could not have been the cup of physical suffering that he had in mind—evil minds have concocted fiendish tortures far more terrible than the crucifixion. He was not afraid of that but he was seeking some way to justify the sovereign power of God other than through the defeat of the cross; he was seeking some way in which he might triumph over evil rather than suffer it. All along he had known this temptation even though he had repulsed it; and knowing how great this temptation could be, he tried to prepare his disciples for it. "Blessed are ye," he said; "blessed are ye when men shall persecute you and betray you and bring you before magistrates and accuse you falsely for my sake. Blessed are you."

And yet how ill-prepared they proved to be when that crucifixion overtook them! Most of them were sure that he would declare himself and call upon the legions of heaven to overcome the evil forces which opposed him. Peter was sure that the goodness of Jesus would insure his triumph. The thought that it might lead to a cross was inconceivable. And it still is for most of us, is it not? We simply cannot understand how it is that goodness should not reign. We think of the power of goodness as a power to dominate and destroy evil, not to suffer it. We ought to be able to call down fire from heaven.

In a world like ours, where evil is rampant and goodness so often at its mercy, the ultimate heart of suffering and the ultimate torture of temptation is to have to face God's reluctance to smite evil—to have to face it and suffer it, seemingly bereft of God's might. Perhaps that is what lay behind Jesus' final struggle with that temptation on the cross when he cried out in agony, "My God, my God, hast thou also forsaken me? Must I face evil alone and possibly go down to defeat before it, or art thou there?"

That is the final temptation—to doubt the final power of love to meet evil, naked and unarmed, except by goodness and courage and faith in God. That is where we come to final grips with doubt. That is where the heart of the world's doubt lies. We cannot believe that love is able to meet evil alone and unafraid because the power of God is in it as Jesus proved. And so our fear drives us to seek some other means in which to put our faith. We are so faithless and so fearful that goodness itself cannot meet evil and will be betrayed and futile, that we frantically lay hold of everything we can find in order to smite evil rather than to face it with goodness.

We would rather be sure of ourselves than be sure of God.

That does not mean that we should not put forth effort to combat evil or that we should throw away our arms or destroy our bank accounts; but it does mean that we should realize that these are not adequate means or ultimate means by which we can ever meet evil's onslaught, that we cannot rest our ultimate faith in them, or resort to evil's tactics, or despair in the face of injustice and failure and frustration. The battle is really on another front where a cross is an instrument of power. That is what Jesus was talking about, and in the end his faith triumphed.

And so on that night when he was betrayed—betrayed by Judas, betrayed by life's experience, betrayed, if you will, by destiny, and seemingly even betrayed by goodness into the hands of evil—Jesus took bread and brake it, a token that he accepted his broken destiny, his broken mission, his broken life, as within the plan of God: God would use his suffering for life's redemption.

On that same night in which he was betrayed, he took bread and brake it; he accepted it for what it stood for, and said, "This is my body broken to redeem through sacrifice, through facing and suffering all that evil can do. In my life's very betrayal lies its mission, in its very failure, its power, in its very defeat, its triumph." That is what he was declaring. For evil can never destroy the life that faces it with courage and with faith in God's grace. This triumph in Christ insists that the spirit of Christ is still an effective instrument in the hands of God with which to meet life's evil forces. He has overcome the world's evil.

Life has no frustrating power that God cannot use, does not use, to bring life's redemption through that cross. "This do in remembrance of me," he says. "Life cannot break you, cannot betray you, cannot frustrate God's purposes in you if you will let God's purposes be fulfilled in your broken, suffering, betrayed experiences.

"Take in your hands life's suffering and defeat, born of loyalty to me," he says, "as I take this broken bread and this cup of my crushed life poured out. Do not hold back! What you suffer in loyalty to me will become a source of God's power for you and for the world. Accept it and let God use it in you and in your life."

And it is in such a spirit and such a loyalty and such a faith that the Christian must meet life. Surely that is the message that comes to us through that table in the Upper Room.

THE LAMB OF GOD

"Behold the Lamb of God, which taketh away the sins of the world."   *John 1:29*

THERE WERE MANY TITLES that were applied to Jesus by those in the New Testament. He was called the Word, the Messiah, Son of Man, the Elder Brother, the Advocate. But perhaps none is as meaningful and appropriate for this season of the year as that given him by John the Baptist when he pointed to Jesus and exclaimed to his disciples, "Behold the Lamb of God, which taketh away the sins of the world."

Although there is no passage in Levitical scripture, or in fact anywhere in the Pentateuch itself, that states that a lamb should be considered as an offering for sin, nevertheless John's hearers were too familiar with the imagery of Isaiah 53 not to understand what he meant to say. It was the audacious magnitude of the idea which was astounding. "Behold the Lamb of God, which taketh away the sins of the world."

There are three messages centered in these words. The first word is "Behold."

Look at him, do not avoid him. See this thing for what it is. Do not blink it or ignore it. Face it! It is the love of God there on that cross, slain like a lamb because evil is real and does things like that. It is ruthless and penetrates men's hearts and their lives and their institutions to work its will. It crucifies. It kills. It destroys. We might as well face that and admit it. "Behold it for what it is," says John. Before the Lamb of God takes away the world's sin he uncovers it for what it is. He makes us see it for what it does to life, through us.

Now that is not the world's way. Instead we try to cover it up, to hide it, to reason it out of existence, to camouflage it. A friend who saw Buchenwald from the inside tells how the walks that led up to the gas chambers were beautifully lined with flowering plants and the gas chambers themselves attractively decorated, outside. There is no evil so dangerous as the evil which justifies itself as good.

Mr. Ogden Reid, who has made a study of the subversive forces in our American life, tells how the most dangerous and treacherous leaders of the Communist Party in the United States belied their seditious allegiance and intentions by masquerading as good citizens and taking an active and seemingly responsible part in church life and Rotary clubs and Masonic lodges and community projects. Evil would always like to pose as an angel of light, to cover itself with sweet righteous reasonableness.

And so we call our evil anything but evil. We call it compromise or expediency or immaturity. But the Word of God in Christ uncovers it and reveals its pernicious pertinence to life. And the first honest act is to behold it for what it is, to admit what it does, to recognize that it puts goodness on a cross, and slashes love across the face, and sneers at it in its heart; that it takes the innocent Lamb and leads him to the slaughter.

And so the first word is "Behold what evil does to the Lamb of God"—the love of God. It puts him upon a cross.

And the second word for us lies in these words, "Lamb of God." This is not an ordinary lamb. There is something cosmic going on here. It is not a mere crucifixion like many other crucifixions. God is in this. This is the Lamb *of God!*

It takes the action of God to make our hearts and our world right. We cannot do it ourselves; it is beyond our powers. Something radical must be done. "O wretched man that I am! Who shall deliver me?" cried Paul. He knew he could not deliver himself. No man has and no nation. The best we have been able to do about sin is to diagnose it.

To be sure, it is not a simple matter. There are many reasons and forces behind our sin, inauspicious economic circumstance, emotional conditioning, threats and anxiety and fear and frustration pushing us on; and compulsions to become persons, to achieve individuality, to find a place for ourselves; compulsions even to be good which end in pride and then deviltry by way of compensation. But whatever inadequacy or whatever drive brings us into it, we are in it up to our necks, ruining our lives, and what is worse, the lives of those about us and our world.

And it is not something we can fix in a moment with a little adjustment here and a little shift of things there. It is deep in the heart of life. Quite possibly the first disciples when they thought over what had happened in Jerusalem and on Calvary may have deplored the unfortunate sequence of events that happened to bring about the crucifixion. There seemed so many places where a slight difference in conditions might have made a vast difference in events; if only he had not aroused the anger of the temple rulers; if only there had been no Judas in their group; if only the rabble had not been stirred up to call for the release of Barabbas instead of Jesus; if only Joseph of Arimathea and Nicodemus had had more power; if only the leaders had been of another stripe. No doubt they saw it as something which could have been avoided, if only someone else had been in the High Priest's chair, or someone else more understanding and courageous had been in Pilate's seat. They did not see that this was a cosmic drama in which Christ was taking part, that it was not just another situation which might have been avoided if circumstances had been otherwise. They did not see that the whole world would have had to be changed to save Christ from the cross, that it required the action of God to meet the situation. This was the Lamb of God because it required divine action to take away our sin. That is the second word for us here.

But there is another word, a triumphant word, for the end is triumph, not tragedy. "He taketh away *the sin* of the world"—not the guilt only, but the sin. He takes our sin away; he nullifies it; he puts something else in its place.

We must not look at that cross and get discouraged. There is a tendency today to think too much of the impalement of God on the cross of evil, to cringe before the power of evil, to doubt the possibility of God's being able to do anything about evil—about communism and fascism and obscurantism and intolerance and hydrogen bombs, and espionage and suspicion and corruption and mass sadism and many other things that harass our modern life—to feel that God is caught in the hands of evil and impaled upon a cross. He was impaled but he was not a victim. He was a victor, and not only at Easter, though of course that is part of it. On that cross and through it he was a transforming power, accepting it and by his very acceptance of it transforming it, proving once and for all that love can accept and suffer all that evil can inflict. Love can go to the cross and then transform it into an instrument to take away evil's power. Love can take everything that evil has laid hold of—men's hearts and hopes and ambitions and powers, temporal powers in state and government, religious powers in church and hierarchy, scientific powers in misused knowledge and skill—love can take all of these in humble acceptance of them and their power, and can permeate them and use them as instruments of God because love is triumphantly transforming.

That is what the Lamb of God does on a cross. We cannot understand it; all we can do is to accept it. But it is real. It reveals to us the Lamb of God taking upon himself all that evil could do and accepting it. He accepts the whole floodgate stream of it, letting it take him without protest and without retaliation, capitulating as it were to all except its method and spirit. He gives himself in utter loyalty to the demand of the Father that love be brought face to face with evil—not give way to it by becoming like it, but always being true to love, always confident that love is God in action. And if we will take hold of it and let it take hold of us, and accept its suffering, we too shall find that love can overcome the power of evil and strip it of its effectiveness.

The Lamb of God even on a cross, indeed because he is on a cross, can defeat evil in its own stronghold where it is trying to do its worst, and can do this because he is the love of God. Love is afraid of nothing, not even a cross. Helpless and unprotected, slain upon the cross he accepts, the Lamb of God transmutes that cross into an instrument for redemption that takes away the sin of the world by that very act! That is why he is the Lamb of God.

But this message is not merely a declaration of a fact

of nineteen hundred years ago. It must be for us an existential fact. That fact in him must become, through him, a fact in us. It is necessary to turn the credo about the Lamb of God into a confirming experience of that sacrificial love, else all our belief is futile. We must let him incorporate that love in ourselves and share his spirit of dynamic redemptive love, and accept its consequences, its crosses if need be. And so out of the depth of our experience we become convinced of his power to take away the sin of the world and we know! We have lived deep enough in it to really know. That is the challenge of the Last Supper, to accept and share that sacrificial love until it becomes a triumphant reality in us by his grace. "This is life eternal that we should know God" through Jesus Christ and share in his redemptive Passion.

✦ ✦ ✦ Good Friday

"WERE YOU THERE?"

*And when they came to the place which is called The
Skull, there they crucified him.*   Luke 23:33

C. F. ANDREWS tells of an experience he had with Dame
Clara Butt, the famous singer. After a severe bereavement,
she had gone to India to find peace and rest and she sought
solace at the ashram of the great poet Rabindranath Tagore,
whose poems had often brought her inspiration and comfort.

She found the poet recovering from a serious illness himself but he welcomed her to his home and they had many
long talks together. At length the time came when she should
return to England. On the night before leaving she, Andrews,
and Tagore sat out on the veranda under the stars, the poet,
still an invalid, reclining on a couch. Dame Clara told him
how much he had helped her and how grateful she was,
and then she said that she still had one more request: could
she sing him a song before going? Of course the poet was
delighted and Mr. Andrews waited with much interest to
see what song she had chosen. And then, in the calm of the

evening, the words of an old Negro spiritual floated out upon the clear air:

> Were you there when they crucified my Lord?
>   Were you there? . . .
> Oh, sometimes my heart begins to tremble.
>   Were you there when they crucified my Lord?

And Mr. Andrews says that he will never forget that song as it was sung there under the stars in the seclusion of the ashram, and the quiet stillness that held all the air when she had finished. When he had retired he lay awake long past midnight thinking of the song and the scene it referred to—the scene at Calvary that had taken place under those same stars. And he wondered if he would have had the courage to stand by the Master's side, not when the crowds were shouting "Hosanna," but when the wild mob was crying, "Crucify him," and when his pierced hands and feet were dripping crimson lifeblood. The words haunted him, "Were you there when they crucified my Lord?" And that is the question which we must ask. Were we there?

In a sense we were all there for Calvary was not simply an event in time—it is the eternal contemporary drama of the tension between redemptive love and evil, and we are always there, on one side or the other.

We were all of us there in so far as we have shared the spirit of those who took a part in it. When we too are like them, then we were there. We cannot escape our responsibility for it simply by an accident of time.

Who was there that first Good Friday?

Stupidity was there—dull, blind, bigoted stupidity. Stupidity is always there when men reject the best and choose the worst. It was stupidity that put Jeremiah in chains and cast him into the pit; stupidity gave Socrates the hemlock to drink, and burned John Huss and Joan of Arc; stupidity assassinated Abraham Lincoln, the best friend the South ever had; stupidity repudiated Wilson and kept us out of the League of Nations; stupidity gave the power to Adolf Hitler and ruined Germany; and stupidity, supported by pride and prejudice and little convictions that blinded them to the greater truth because they were so sure they were right, led the authorities to crucify the fairest, truest, bravest, noblest spirit that the world has ever known. The destiny of a people hung in that decision, and blind stupidity led men to repudiate the one way out. Yes, stupidity was there. Cowardly stupidity is always on hand at crucifixions. Will our own complacent blindness bring the same tragedy to our day?

Fear was there, fear of truth, fear of new ideas, fear of new ways, fear of change, and fear of goodness that always breeds intolerance. Fear was there, fear that fanned the flames of hatred, for men hate what they fear, and the measure of their hatred is the measure of their fear. Fear was there, fear that sought protection behind swords and pikes and strong-arm methods. Fear knows no reason; its only method is force. Fear hides behind prejudice that it calls convictions and arms itself with autocratic power and ruthless authority. It dares not trust to anything else.

And because fear was there, cruelty was there. Cruelty plaited a crown of thorns and crushed it on his brow; cruelty threw a purple robe around his shoulders and thrust a reed in his hands and spat in his face and laughed with scorn, in a vain attempt to break his spirit. Cruelty cried, "Crucify him! Crucify him!" and drove hard nails through his hands and feet, and let him hang through the long, sweltering hours of the heat of the day, with swollen, festering, blood-caked wounds. Cruelty was there—cruelty that began with selfish carelessness and ended in malicious torture; cruelty that started with thoughtless ridicule and ended with blows. Cruelty was there—cruelty that was sustained by righteous

indignation in the hearts of priests and by self-justification
in the hearts of the authorities, and by a sense of duty in
the hearts of the soldiers. But always cruelty, nevertheless,
heartless cruelty in the end. And it is always cruelty that
results when one wants one's own way of thinking or one's
own way of doing things or one's own way of getting things
at any cost. Cruelty maintained slavery, kept little children
in factories and men and women in concentration camps;
cruelty drove the loyal Japanese out of their homes and stores
in America; cruelty sent hundreds of thousands of refugees
to the gas chamber. Talk about the crucifixion being contemporary! Cruelty lets children starve and thrusts deportees
into an unwelcome world, and persecutes men because of
their color, and ignores men in their hour of need.

And indifference was there. The record says, "The bystanders sat and watched him there." "One more misguided
enthusiast come to grief. Too bad," they said. "One more
idealist who wanted to change things, put out of the way by
the powers that be. Too bad it had to happen, but it's no
affair of ours. Every man has to look out for himself."

Life went on just the same as ever the day of the crucifixion; people went on preparing the Passover feast, the
singers went on intoning the chants in the temple, the priests
went on saying prayers to Jehovah, and after the Passover
business went on as usual.

There were only a few who knew anything different:
Peter and James and John and a few disciples, Mary and
Martha and Magdalene and a few others; only a few score,
not many. Yes, indifference was there, as it still is, by the
side of cruelty. Every man who wants things changed for
the better has to face indifference and spiritual inertia, and
to pour out his own lifeblood before men are stirred into
action.

Lust must have been there, angered, outraged lust that

had been frustrated in working its vengeance a short time before. Now the hands that were restrained from grasping the stones they had sought for the woman taken in adultery could be lifted in fisted defiance against the one whose justice and mercy had frustrated their design. The lustful heart is often the quickest and loudest to damn others for what it would like to do itself, and when its means of judgment is thwarted it turns to bigotry and cruelty. Lust must have been there.

Stupidity, fear, lust, cruelty, and indifference were all there; all had a hand in the crucifixion. But that is only one group that was there. There was another. The other side was there also. The picture is not all black.

Hope was there, hope hid in the heart of a brigand who hung on a cross by the Master's side; hope alive and vibrant despite agony. "Master, remember me when thou comest into thy kingdom." Yes, hope was there, hope that goodness would triumph; hope that love would win; and hope that the true Kingdom would come through him.

How his words must have gladdened and thrilled the heart of the Master—"Remember me, when thou comest into thy kingdom." It was a flash of insight that somehow in the midst of all the blood and sweat and tears caught a vision of the eternal significance of Calvary and knew that there was victory there.

Dignity was there. We think of Jesus as the victim on Calvary when he was really the victor. He was in command throughout. He led the way to the cross. The others were forced there as persecutors under the compulsion of their passions and prejudices. He alone was free. From the moment that they took him into custody he was the real master. In the very hour of betrayal he dispensed healing as a giver of gracious mercy. When he stood before his judges, Caiaphas, Pilate, and Herod, every one of them was conscious that it was they who were being tried, not he. He answered them not a word and they marvelled at his silence. It was a silence that hurt. And even on the cross he was in moral command. Instead of imploring mercy at their hands he commended them to forgiveness at the hands of his Father in heaven. There was a royal, inner dignity there. Dignity was there because trust was there, implicit trust, trust that could say, "Not my will but thine be done," trust that could look without fear into the face of death and say, "Father, into thy hands I commend my spirit." Trust is the only way to poise and strength, trust based on unbroken faith, faith that life does not hang on incidents but upon a destiny that rests in the hands of One whose goodness and power can never be thwarted, even by a cross or a sepulcher.

And self-forgetting sacrifice was there, sacrifice that counted not the cost, sacrifice that knew the issues of life. "Except a grain of wheat fall into the ground and die, it abideth alone: but if it die, it bringeth forth much fruit." Here was sacrifice born of love. "Greater love hath no man than this, that a man lay down his life for his friends." "Even as the Son of man came not to be ministered unto but to minister, and to give his life a ransom for many."

The record might have read, as Robb Zaring suggests, "Now before the feast of the Passover, Jesus, knowing that his hour had come . . . began to be suspicious, and during supper, seeing that something was about to happen, the Devil having already put it into the heart of Judas Iscariot, Simon's son, to betray him, Jesus riseth from supper, excuseth himself and goeth out into the night; and in a little while might have been seen fleeing out of the gate through which a week before he had ridden in triumph."

Or again it could have read, "And the whole company of them rose up and brought him before Pilate. And they began to accuse him, saying, 'We found this man perverting our nation.' And Herod and his soldiers set him at naught and mocked him; and they came unto a place which is called The Skull and there they crucified him; and hot anger surged up in his heart and he cried out in rebellion at their cruelty, and he cursed them with a mighty curse."

He might have done that if he were like us, but love and forgiveness were there that day—love that was strong enough to suffer cruelty and hatred without resentment; love that held no malice. And from the agony of the cross what he did say was, "Father, forgive them; they don't know what they are doing."

And through the centuries his closest followers have been those who have lived by that spirit. Men have seen the love that was at Calvary evidenced in the lives of spirits like Horace Pitkin and Eleanor Chestnut and a host of others.

You remember how when Horace Pitkin, the missionary, was about to be killed by the Boxers in China, his last statement to his body-servant was to express his hope that his baby son, who was with his wife in America, might grow up and prepare himself to come back to China to serve these same people who had killed his father.

And Eleanor Chestnut, another sainted missionary, as she was being held prisoner for a moment before being stabbed and thrown into a lake by the Boxers, tore off a part of her dress to stop the flow of a severed artery that one of her captors had suffered.

Or consider the case of the father and mother who on hearing that their two children who were missionaries in the East had been murdered, sold their property and undertook a course of training in order that, at their own expense, they might replace their children.

These are dramatic cases but many others have shared that spirit.

Yes, they were all there, stupidity, fear, lust, cruelty and indifference on the one side, and hope, trust, dignity, self-sacrifice and love and forgiveness on the other. Now the question is: Were *you* there when they crucified the Lord? Where did you stand? Where do you stand?

Suppose we did not know anything about Easter today, this one day; that we could make our choice and take our stand today; that we too could say, "Here I am. I'll take my stand here by him. 'Beneath the cross of Jesus, I fain would take *my* stand!' "

And we can, for after all the question, "Were you there?" does not pertain alone to that far-off scene. For one day we shall be facing the question, "Were you there when they crucified the Lord?" not in A.D. 30 but today. Were you there *then,* when they crucified the Lord? And we shall say, "Where, Lord? When saw we thee crucified?" And He will answer, "I was there. I was imprisoned in ignorance and fear. I was naked and hungry and poverty-stricken. I was unemployed. I was exploited. I was in trouble. I was forsaken, friendless, and discouraged, crucified anew in the sufferings of men. Where were *you* then? Were you there when they crucified your Lord?"

That is the final question!

The Seven Words from the Cross

THE FIRST WORD

"Father, forgive them; for they know not what they do."   Luke 23:34

I T IS DIFFICULT to put into words what Jesus put into a cross. Yet words have their place as well as deeds, and the

words of Christ from the cross may help us to understand
what went on there.

The First Word is no doubt the most familiar and surely
the most quoted of them all:

"Father, forgive them; for they know not what they do."

This is one of the most comforting passages in all the
New Testament, not only because it moves us deeply with
its vision of a magnanimous spirit, stooping to a generous
gesture towards his persecutors in the midst of his agony, but
particularly because it reveals to us the depth of his redemptive Passion.

I am not sure that Jesus himself completely understood
all that his cross meant, but he knew within him that God
was accomplishing something through it mightier than he
had ever done on earth before. Something was happening at
Golgotha that should determine the destiny of men forever
after. It was a cosmic crisis.

The age-long struggle between evil and goodness had
come to a focus in mortal combat on that cross! Love was
finally declaring its power; evil was doing its worst. It was
a spiritual event of epochal proportions, and yet those who
witnessed it seemed totally blind to what was going on, as we
so often are, and it is here that is revealed the depth of the
Master's Passion. Certainly the burden of his prayer was for
forgiveness for all who had a part in his crucifixion, but it
was particularly and especially for those who had not the wit
to see what they were doing.

"Father, forgive them," he pleads, "for they know not
what they do."

It's that last bit that makes that prayer so precious, because it includes us all!

The remarkable nature of this prayer stands out as one
considers the groups gathered around that cross: the curious
people standing dumbly by, morbidly watching, twisting their
faces in grimaces and sucking in their breath between their

teeth over some paroxysm of agony; the gaming soldiers hardened and callous to the taking of life, seeking cruel sport in mocking and ridiculing and trying to bait him; the chief priests and rulers, scoffing and scorning and wagging their heads in derision; all, without exception, completely oblivious to what was really going on! I think this wanton blindness of heart must have been the hardest thing for Jesus to bear.

No one, except the penitent thief, raised a voice in his favor. No one seemed to protest; and still more tragic, no one seemed to shudder in his heart over the warped and desperate state of soul of those who could perpetrate such deeds. No doubt there were some who sorrowed, but they sorrowed over the suffering Jesus endured, not over the tragedy of soul of those who could so indifferently inflict it.

Only Jesus seemed to have felt this. He knew that they, and not he, were the ones to be pitied. It wasn't the pain that they inflicted upon him that hurt him so much as the condition to which their folly and stupidity had brought them, the evil that had caught up with them and taken possession of them, and left them blind to all goodness.

He knew that the greatest tragedy that can overtake a soul is to come to the point where sin no longer hurts, and cruelty no longer shocks, and evil no longer is hateful, and goodness no longer stirs one's heart to admiration and joy and hope. Spiritual leprosy had overtaken them.

They tell us that the great tragedy for the leper comes when his fingers no longer have a sense of feeling and he burns them irreparably in the flame over which he cooks his food. So these men had become the witless servants of evil, never realizing that it was evil. Their spiritual compromise and evil entanglements had deadened their souls both to what was good and what was evil until they didn't know one from the other. And so, as Jesus said, they did not know what they were doing.

There was nothing they could do. There was nothing in them for his goodness to make any impression on, nothing solid enough in their lives for goodness to get a foothold on, and so they ended by either letting him be killed or taking a hand in it. That was a condition which cried for God's mercy, for only he could do anything in such a case. And Jesus, who loved all men, both good and bad, just couldn't stand that without crying out from the depths of his soul for God's mercy and forgiveness for them; their tragedy was so deep and so terrible.

And so it is a very comforting prayer for us, because I think that perhaps our greatest danger lies in our unrecognized sins, which we cherish blindly.

What we see and know and do we can at least repent of and shun, but what we do not see or recognize is what betrays and damns our souls, because it confirms us in our self-righteousness.

For the most part these people around the cross were convinced that they were doing what was right, or at least they felt that duty justified the evil they were forced to do, or that circumstances made it inevitable. The result was that they had become inured to evil until they thought of it as good and were blind and deaf and unfeeling in its presence!

That's a tragic situation. The tragedy wasn't that they were crucifying the Son of God. The tragedy was that they were crucifying, period—that they could crucify anyone heartlessly.

There are two ways by which we fall into this tragic condition. One is by our neglect of goodness, our carelessness of goodness, our reluctance to keep our spirits sensitive to new implications of goodness through increasing contact with the mind and spirit of Christ. And so we become satisfied with the little Christ we want and blind to the real Christ, and we betray him without knowing it. We know not what we do!

Few of us know what we do when it comes to Jesus. Our loyalty is so feeble, our comprehension so fragmentary, our love so poorly implemented. It is there that most Christians stand in need of forgiveness, not for the disgraceful sins which all men condemn and we repent of. The discipline of Christian idealism generally prevents sin of voluntary commission, but our reluctant sensitivity to Christ opens our lives to a host of deadlier sins born of our willful ignorance! If we knew what we were doing we should be appalled, but we do not and we go on our way satisfied with our superficial discipleship, not realizing that we are crucifying his spirit in a thousand stupid ways.

That is one way in which we become entangled in unknown evil, and the other way is by our unreluctant involvement in an evil system of things, our real, if unconscious, conformity to the kingdom of Antichrist.

It's our willing compromise with evil that damns us, our acceptance of wrong under the pressure of necessity or policy or prudence until we finally espouse it as good. Public opinion, for instance, or propaganda, makes us hate the Russians until at last we think it is right to hate Russians; or we find ourselves under the necessity of meeting force with greater force until finally we find ourselves declaring that force is the right way to overcome evil!

Caught in the complications of evil systems from which we cannot extricate ourselves, we give up and capitulate to evil, and finally grasp it to our hearts and accept it as good. We would rather be consistent than confess our evil plight and our need of a Saviour. That is a temptation which is very acute today.

Those Roman soldiers who set up the cross were doing their duty. Cruelty had become their profession. Perhaps they had been conscripted and could do nothing about it and so had blunted their hearts against the horror of torture. They had no feeling against Jesus personally; they probably knew very little about him, but they had become accustomed to cruelty. It was their way of adjusting to an evil lot. So their consciences could no longer function, their hearts could no longer bleed with sympathy. You see, they had become the victims both of their own callousness and of a hard, thoughtless and uncaring system!

That bespeaks so much of the situation in which we find ourselves that it is doubly comforting to know that the forgiveness of God goes out to the unwitting sins in which we have become involved in our unchristian world. Not that such forgiveness should make us condone the folly of our ignorant sin—far from it! Instead we should face it and see it for what it is, and not harden our hearts to it but confess it!

How often we accept practices in our personal life, or in affairs of statecraft or society, which necessity dictates and which we know are wrong and yet inwardly accept until we are so mixed up we no longer know what is right and what is wrong! We are confused and know not what we do. That is when we need forgiveness the most, when we need heart-healing the most, for it is only when we are forgiven and hear God's word again that we can see aright and know what we should do. Only through forgiveness can we again see clearly and be free from the confusion of soul that blinds us.

And so it is good for us at Passion time to face the cross with the suffering Christ hanging upon it and let it cut in upon our complacent discipleship and rebuke our hearts until we make his prayer our prayer, changing it to make us say, as we ought to say:

"Father, forgive us; we know not what we do!"

THE SECOND WORD

"To-day shalt thou be with me in paradise."   Luke
23:43

"Two others also, who were criminals, were led away
to be put to death with him. And when they came to the
place which is called The Skull, there they crucified him, and
the criminals one on the right and one on the left. . . . And
the people stood by, watching; but the rulers scoffed at him,
saying, 'He saved others; let him save himself, if he is the
Christ of God, His Chosen One!' The soldiers also mocked
him . . . saying, 'If you are the King of the Jews, save yourself!'

"One of the criminals who were hanged railed at him,
saying, 'Are you not the Christ? Save yourself and us!' But
the other rebuked him, saying, 'Do you not fear God, since
you are under the same sentence of condemnation? And we
justly; for we are receiving the due reward of our deeds; but
this man has done nothing wrong!' And he said, 'Jesus, remember me when you come into your kingly power.' And
he said to him, 'Truly, I say to you, today you will be with
me in Paradise.' "

The crucifixion scene is a study in contrasts!

There is the agony of those upon the crosses on the one
hand, and the cruel indifference of the executioners
on the other.

The vindictive sneers of the rulers and the forgiving
spirit of Jesus!

The weeping, heart-broken women bowed in grief and
the careless soldiers throwing dice for his robe!

The animosity of the chief priests and the admiration
of the Roman centurion!

The Man Christ hanging upon the cross, paying the
price of man's sin and the idle bystanders looking on
as indifferent spectators!

Striking contrasts, all of them!

But these contrasts which characterized this scene are
nowhere more evident than in the case of the two thieves,
for the cross that stood between them thrust them worlds
apart!

The one was damned by the bitterness that it brought
to his soul, the other was saved by the hope that it aroused
within his.

One railed on Christ for his impotence, and one blessed
him for his compassion!

One passed into perdition with cynical curses on his
lips, and the other stepped into paradise with a new light in
his soul.

They suffered together but the suffering of the one thrust
him forever from Christ's side and the suffering of the other
drew him forever into his presence.

We know little about these two robbers! An old manuscript calls them Dysmas and Gestus, the penitent and the
unpenitent. Perhaps they were mere brigands—the moun-
tains of Judea were infested with bands of outlaws who had
become bandits—or they may have been revolutionaries of
the Judean resistance! In any case, the crucifixion of Jesus
became the occasion for them to join him at Calvary, and
in that meeting, tragic though it was, their destinies were
fixed, as is so often the case when men meet Christ in the hour
of crisis. Gestus, tortured perhaps beyond endurance, burst

out into vilification; Dysmas, moved to penitence, sued for mercy.

Those are the bare facts, little enough, and yet they reveal the motives that dominated their lives.

Perhaps it would seem unfair to judge anyone's reaction under such terribly agonizing conditions. Prolonged public torture such as they were suffering would seem excruciating enough to distort any thought or action born of such torment. And yet those two malefactors were judged out of their own hearts. On the face of it the bitter blasphemous cry of Gestus may seem to have been wrung from his lips in the desperate defiance of despair born of the darkness of his dying hour; but men's reactions in the time of crisis are always the result of the dominant trend of their souls. And the source of this cynical outburst was more deep-seated than the suffering of the moment. Often under the stress of pressure, men reveal their deepest feelings, and so with this robber.

The churlish sneer that colored his outburst was evidence of what he thought of Jesus. "If thou be the Christ, prove it by force and power." The only argument that he knew was the argument of hard steel and overpowering might. If its testimony was lacking, it was folly to count on mere goodness of heart or sacrifice to effect victory! If Jesus could not triumph over his foes by a display of power, as very evidently he could not, then he was no Christ, but a weak impostor. The only proof Gestus recognized was command of overwhelming power. If Jesus could not resort to power to prove his Messiahship, he had no claim to it. His very defeat was a sign and proof of his false pretensions, his incompetence. Gestus simply couldn't conceive of a king on a cross, unless it was a defeated, repudiated, dethroned king. From his viewpoint, it was utterly idiotic to suffer evil if one could destroy it by force.

And yet at heart that's the way a great many of us feel, isn't it? We think of the power of goodness as a power to dominate and destroy evil, not to suffer it. On the face of it, there is very little in a broken, bloody, lonely figure on a cross, suffering evil to work its way with it, to inspire hope. If he was really the Son of God, he ought to have been able to smite evil, not to suffer it.

That's where we come to final grips with doubt, isn't it? For that's where the heart of the world's doubt lies. We can't believe that love is able, if need be, to meet evil, naked and unafraid, because it has the power of God in it. And so our fear drives us to seek material security and physical force in which to put our faith. We are so fearful that goodness in itself does not have the power to meet evil but will be betrayed and futile, that we frantically lay hold of the security of material things and seek the strength of might and physical power in order to smite evil rather than to face it with the weapons of God. As we said before, we would rather be sure of ourselves than be sure of God.

Please don't misunderstand me. This does not mean that we should abolish all tangible means of combating evil. But we must realize that these alone are no match for the failures and despair to which total dependency upon them can ultimately lead.

Gestus personifies this despair. Failure had turned him cynical. He hadn't the remotest thought that Jesus could save either himself or them. He not only scorned the power of such goodness but he scorned the reality of it. All goodness was hollow and unreal. He had no desire for it. Under other circumstances he would have boasted that he was a practical man, that he wanted no dreams that could not be realized in the rough-and-ready world in which he lived. He had no interest in a Kingdom of Heaven. Now, facing the bitter reality of failure, he cursed life as a fraud.

This cynical thief is typical of all who twist life's values until they no longer can recognize goodness for what it is. He would rather cling to his own bitter appraisal of life and the world and destiny than admit God's goodness and accept His Grace. To him the cross on which Jesus hung had no more significance than his own. It stood for failure, weakness and ultimate defeat, all things he despised. Such goodness as Jesus' had no place in a realistic world and deserved none. It had no meaning for him. He and Jesus had nothing in common except a common condemnation. The gracious spirit who shrank not from the cross and paid the last drop of blood that man's sin required, who never capitulated to hatred or gave way to vindictive protest, won from him no admiration. He had no faith in goodness or in the cosmic power of vicarious sacrifice.

This man who hung beside him did not speak to him of the Divine. His gracious words of forgiveness touched no responsive chord in his heart, brought no echo of God's compassion to his ears, no vision of mercy to his soul. From his standpoint, both of them were victims of the ultimate senselessness of the universe.

He had lost all sensitivity to goodness, and so he did not see the poverty of his own soul or feel the need of mercy, and thus he cherished no hope. Let the others talk of heaven if they wished; it was all damned foolishness to him. And that was his damnation, for the one who stands in the presence of goodness and despises it, and misinterprets it and the heart of the universe in which it is grounded, damns himself because he has denatured the universe and dethroned the love and goodness and holiness of God. By so doing, he has repudiated all moral reality and so all opportunity for his own salvation. That's why Jesus' cross meant nothing to him.

There are some persons whom even the Cross cannot

touch, upon whose hearts such goodness can find no place to get a foothold. There is no heaven for them because they do not want or believe in heaven. That is the tragedy of Gestus.

But consider for a moment the thief who hung on the other side. Remember he too was hanging upon a cruel cross, under the same condemnation, suffering the same agonies, facing the same bitter end. And yet, as Robertson Nicoll has said, this man Dysmas "was the only one in all the world who really believed in Jesus at that moment." All the others were disillusioned, fear-bound and hopeless. Only this thief who hung on a cross by his side had faith enough in this broken, bleeding, wounded, defeated, fly-infested figure to believe that one day he should inherit a Kingdom. Such a faith could only be born in the heart of one who, though he lived in sin, still believed in goodness and so could see and recognize the royal imprint of ineffable goodness on this blood-stained face. The vision of one who, though he was reviled, reviled not again, who, though he was tortured and mocked, gave vent to no vindictive bitterness, who, though he was grieviously mistreated, offered only forgiveness, smote his heart to penitence.

He was the true realist, not the other. He knew that he had done wrong, that a just punishment had overtaken him. He neither belittled his sin nor denied his guilt; instead he accepted his punishment as the equitable price that he must pay. Deep within his heart there was a recognition of the essential moral quality of life and of the world.

He had rebelled against the law of God and was suffering a fair punishment for his sin. He blamed no one but himself. "We suffer justly," he admitted. He did not excuse himself by putting it off on his ancestors or his environment or his own unhappy ignorance or finite weakness.

And because he recognized his own evil he was able

to recognize Jesus' goodness which the others could not. This man who hung beside him with the crown of thorns on his brow was of another order. He belonged to the Kingdom of God. From his lips words of mercy had meaning and authority. Dysmas had never rationalized either sin or goodness out of existence as Gestus had done.

He believed in the righteousness of God, and Jesus made it possible for him to believe in the compassion of God.

He held no theory of the atonement, knew no doctrine of the Cross, but he saw the mercy of God in the man who hung upon it.

He still believed, despite his own failure and sin, in a God of righteousness, and still believed that evil and sin merited judgment, that goodness would reign, even from a cross. And despite his own failure Jesus had made him so confident of the ultimate triumph of goodness and so confident of the mercy of God that in the midst of his misery of heart, born not so much of his pain of body as of his penitence of spirit, he turned to Jesus and pled with him. "Master, remember me when thou comest into thy kingdom as thou surely will—remember me."

And Jesus, conscious no doubt that here was the first fruit of his redemptive Passion, with characteristic compassion, turned to him and said, "Verily, I say unto thee, today shalt thou be with me in paradise."

For Paradise is open to those who, conscious of their sin and guilt, hunger and thirst after righteousness and seek the mercy of God through Christ. While those who clothe themselves in pride and feel no need of Christ, forever shut themselves outside.

THE THIRD WORD

"Woman, behold thy son! . . . Behold thy mother!"
John 19:26, 27

THIS IS A DEEPLY MOVING SCENE. On the face of it we all
wonder at the compassionate thoughtfulness of one who
stops in the midst of his consuming agony to show such
tender care for his mother, to make sure that she shall have
a roof over her head and kindness in her old age. One could
sentimentalize over it at great length, as some indeed have
done.

But when one stops to consider the facts one wonders
more deeply. The fact is Mary was not childless. Jesus had
brothers and sisters amply able to take care of their mother.
James, her next-born, was well known. No doubt it was he
who had taken over the carpenter shop when Jesus had left
it. Moreover there is no reason to think that her daughters,
mentioned by Mark, could not have taken her home with
them and provided for her.

There must have been some deeper reason which lay
behind this compassionate commission to John. Perhaps we
get a clue to it when we remember that for all of her love
for him, Mary had never really understood her son. We
tend to romanticize the situation. Mary does not seem to
have been one of Jesus' early followers. She was undoubtedly
a lovely person but she seems to have been bothered by
doubts about her son's actions and sanity. There were times
when she thought him beside himself. Perhaps she found

it hard to reconcile herself to the drastic course he had taken. There is more than a little indication that something of a rift had grown up between himself and his family. Witness his abrupt response to his mother at the marriage in Cana, saying what was equivalent to, "Mother, you keep out of this." And the emphasis he put upon the necessity of a man's forsaking his home and family. His comment that a man's foes might be those of his own household may very well have been born of his own experience. You remember how on one occasion when they told him that his mother and brothers were without seeking him, he broke out almost impatiently: "But who are my mother and my brothers?" And then drawing a distinction between those of his family without and those who were listening to his preaching, he said pointing to the latter, "These are my mother and my brothers, these who do the will of God."

And again when his fellow-townsmen would not receive or hear him, he not only quoted the familiar proverb about a prophet being without honor in his own country, but he added "And in his own household where" as he had said before, "a man's enemies may very well be found."

All of these are indicative of a certain lack of harmony in the family circle. It seems evident that Jesus considered spiritual ties closer than blood-ties.

In such a situation if he were concerned for the spiritual welfare of his mother, the family could not provide it. Her family could have taken care of her bodily needs quite adequately. It was her spiritual needs, so intensified in this hour, that they could not care for. The atmosphere of the family would hardly be the place for her. She would need a deeper, more understanding and sustaining fellowship to see her through this trying ordeal and to bring her to the point where she could finally understand him and see why he had done what he had done, and above all why he had let this terrible destiny come upon him, which no one understood.

It is not surprising that his family did not understand him. Jesus' whole life was haunted by misunderstanding. The people mistook him time and time again.

The rulers mistook him for an ambitious, revolutionary upstart who threatened their hold of power and privilege. And in a way they were right. The Pharisees and chief priests mistook him for a misguided reformer who might undermine their whole religious system. And in a sense they were right too. The zealots mistook him for the deliverer who would free them from the bondage of Rome by setting up an earthly kingdom. And still others mistook him for a miracle-man who could provide them with food and security.

No doubt Judas thought that as the Christ, Jesus would be impervious to Caiaphas' scheming and Pilate's power and if betrayed would call upon the legions of angels. Peter thought Jesus' role and destiny would preclude any possibility of his submitting to a cross as beneath his station. James and John thought that he would inaugurate a divine reign on a throne, on either side of which they two might sit. The crowd of pilgrims on Palm Sunday thought that he would take over the reins of government and achieve a coup d'état.

Few believed in him for what he was. And when he actually died on a cross, they thought it was all over, a horrible tragedy of failure. They had counted on him to restore Israel. But he had failed. None of them was prepared for the kind of triumph that came. Easter was furthest from their minds or hopes.

And we still misunderstand him, and try to make him the master of our lives as we want them, not as he wants them. But he escapes us and goes his way, which is God's way. And the only way that we can ever understand him and

see him for what he is, is by the way of obedience and love
and fellowship. And that is why Jesus commended his mother
to John. The others in her family could not be of any help
here.

Mary needed an understanding heart to stay her. The
crucifixion was a terrible experience for her to face, as you
can imagine. All her mother-love and deep affection must
have welled up in yearning for her son. What memories
must have flooded her heart! She must have gone back in
her memory to the time of his birth when he had been
wrapped in swaddling clothes and lain in a manger, and of
the portents of a destiny which events had never fulfilled.
Somehow he had missed it. Again her memory must have
gone back to the happy days of his childhood when he played
among the chips and sawdust of his father's carpenter shop.
She had watched him grow into developing boyhood, helping his father and roaming the hills revelling in the beauties
of nature. She must have thought too of the family journey
to Jerusalem and of his eagerness to learn.

All through the years her love had followed him, her
first-born, even though she had not understood him. Then
came the time when he had laid down his saw and hammer,
and breaking away, had gone out to preach. She must have
been troubled by the almost rebel strangeness and boldness
of his teaching and his audacious clashes with the authorities. She remembered how perturbed she had been and how
embarrassed when he shocked their respectable neighbors
with his bold doctrine. To be sure she rejoiced over his
healing ministry and his gentle tenderness with children
and the helpless, but his unconventional, disreputable as-
sociations and his unorthodox way of ignoring religious tradi-
tion and custom troubled her.

Nevertheless a mother's love sweeps all that aside in its

deep, warm feeling and wells up strong and loyal in any hour of crisis. And this was a terrible crisis for them both.

The horror of the cross must have torn at her breast. She was too tender-hearted not to wince with misery at the sight of any cross. Now it was her own son who hung on this one. It was flesh of her flesh that was being tortured. It was a terrible experience for a mother. She might easily have become rebellious and embittered and hurt beyond repair. It might well have meant the end of all her faith. It might have stripped her of her sanity and left her soul twisted and seared beyond healing. Her sense of God's justice and providence might well have been crushed and her heart wrung dry of faith. Many a life has been ruined by a lesser ordeal than she was going through. However puzzled over her son's actions in provoking his fate she may have been, she was a sensitive spirit and that is the kind that suffers most acutely and is most easily unbalanced mentally and spiritually. So sorrow-stricken and perplexed of heart, she stood before that cruel cross upon which her son was impaled, her pain the greater because she could not understand the reason or the meaning of that suffering.

None of them did. It was the cross itself that was to open their eyes and hearts. This cross which was so terrible to them now, was to take on a deep new meaning that should give meaning to all crosses. You see, when Jesus confided his mother to John it was more than an act of filial compassion and concern for her physical welfare. It was concern for her soul, not only her wounded heart. He wanted her to be protected by the warm fellowship of loyal believing hearts, in order that her love for him, so sorely tried, could find its way through to a faith in him and in his Cross.

And I think that Jesus did this both for his mother and for John. They needed each other if their faith was to blossom into understanding and a new loyalty. Mary needed to lean upon John and John needed someone to draw out the latent forces of his soul. Spiritual responsibility is the path to a deepened life and a richer, fuller faith. As we share the spiritual needs of others who may not yet understand as fully as we the depth and meaning of the Gospel, we, ourselves, grow in spiritual grace and understanding: "Loving and being loved," as the Book of Worship says, "we are prepared for the fellowship of Saints above."

And that is one reason for the Church, "The Beloved Community," as they called it, "The Loving Community"— that by sharing our loyalty and sustaining one another, we may grow in spiritual stature through our mutual experience.

Our mutual concern can lead us into a deeper understanding of grace, and our compassion can lead us into a deeper understanding of God's compassion in Christ. Our mutual forgiveness can lead us into a deeper realization of God's forgiveness, and even our suffering can lead us into a deeper understanding of the Cross if we suffer, not only for ourselves, but for others, as did he who "came not to be ministered unto but to minister, and to give his life a ransom for many."

THE FOURTH WORD

"My God, my God, why hast thou forsaken me?"
Matt. 27:46

"Now from the sixth hour there was darkness over all the land unto the ninth hour. And about the ninth hour

Jesus cried with a loud voice, 'Eli, Eli, lama sa-bach-tha-ni?'
—that is, 'My God, my God, why hast thou forsaken me?'
And some of the bystanders hearing it said, 'This man is
calling Elijah.' And one of them at once ran and took a
sponge, filled it with vinegar, and put it on a reed, and gave
it to him to drink." (Matt. 27:45–48 [R.S.V.])

No more poignant words have ever been wrung from
human lips than these words that came from Jesus in the
midst of the crucifixion's torment and torture. "My God, my
God, why hast thou forsaken me?" It seems clear from the
Gospel account that it was not only necessary that Jesus
should suffer the terrible physical agony of a horrible, linger-
ing death, hung by his nailed hands from the beam of a
Roman cross, but that he must also suffer the greater torment
of a spirit given over to doubt and spiritual desolation, that
alone on the cross he should find himself also alone in the
universe, with no answering echo to the love that was within
his own heart.

The fact that these words are actually a quotation from
the Twenty-second Psalm does not in any way take from them
their deep and desperate feeling. They come as the culmina-
tion of an emotion that must have been growing within him.
All great men are truly lonely. Their greatness sets them
apart and the greater they are the greater their fundamental
isolation.

A Christian explorer tells of a conversation which he
had with an old African chief as they sat together around the
fire after all the others had left. The explorer spoke of the
honor that the old man enjoyed as the chief of the tribe. But
the old chief, with many years' experience written on his
wrinkled face, only shook his head and said, "Yes, I am the
chief it is true, but the life of the chief is a lonely one; for
the chief must go down the pathway of life ahead of all the
others where he can have no companions. There's no one

who knows enough to understand the pathway of his thoughts. He must always be alone."

And then he turned his searching eyes upon his companion and said, "Have you ever thought how lonely God must be? And how lonely Jesus must have been? So few understood him."

Almost from the beginning Jesus was misunderstood, with a misunderstanding that grew and inevitably created a widening gulf between him and his hearers. Perhaps it was this widening gulf which bore in upon him the conviction of his Messiahship. He was increasingly aware of the deep difference of his life from that of his fellows and of their almost hopeless incapacity to understand him, their persistent, stubborn desire to cast him in their own mold, to make of him a magician, a soothsayer, a social insurgent, or a revolutionary leader. The fact that he had come to unveil to them a God of love who sought a Kingdom where he should reign in the hearts of men and so redeem them was utterly incomprehensible to them. And even to his disciples, those who lived nearest to him, the thought of a Messiah who should submit rather than dominate, should serve rather than be served, and who should finally suffer and be killed, was unbearable. It is no wonder that as he drew nearer to the cross, he realized that the nearer he came to Calvary the farther he drew from his fellows.

There is a strange significance in a passing comment made by the writer of one of the Gospels. The story of the last night, in Gethsemane, pictures Jesus leading his disciples on guard to watch while he himself went on into the garden and on into the night. And the Evangelist says, "He went on a little further." Those are words which are richly descriptive, for that was particularly distinctive of Christ. He went on when others stopped, on in his loyalty to God and on in his passion to give himself. Not only did he stand out because of the majesty of his goodness—he did more than any other had attempted. He was unique because his goodness went on beyond being good to being a redeemer of men. And finally, it was his Saviourhood that marked his distinction. And in the end that is why his death was unique.

His destiny set him apart. And with the coming of the soldiers he found himself alone, abandoned to an isolation which knew no relief until his death. From then on he was to taste the bitter dregs of his unique aloneness. He was alone before Caiaphas and the Jewish tribunal, alone before Herod, alone in the hands of the soldiers, alone with Pilate, alone even with the crowd who cried "Crucify him!"

At no time could he turn and count upon a friendly smile of understanding, the affectionate calling of his name, the encouraging gesture of the wave of a hand, or a heartening word of an advocate pleading his case. He was alone, always. Later to be sure, on the way to Golgotha, there seemed to be no lack of pity, but pity only intensifies one's sense of loneliness. And on the cross the loneliness of his plight must have increased as the pain set in and, physically weakened by the loss of blood and the rising fever of infection, he felt the full impact of his lonely destiny to suffer more than all the others and to be misunderstood for doing it.

It's hard for us to face that cross realistically as Jesus did; a light shines from it today that it did not have for Jesus. It was not a unique experience to be crucified. Men had died upon crosses before, many of them, but they had always died as criminals, the victims of shame and disapproval. Crucifixion was not an honorable death. It stood for defeat and disgrace. It seemed inconceivable that the will of God could be in it. Even though Jesus himself accepted it as God's purpose, he faced it with deep reluctance.

I feel sure he did not seek or court it, though he seemed

to see clearly its inevitability. He realized that he must face it but he always thought that somehow God would transform it into a triumph. "And I, if I be lifted up from the earth, will draw all men unto me," he said. "Except a grain of wheat fall into the ground and die, it abideth alone: but if it die it bringeth forth much fruit." He seemed to count on God's using it, but as yet there was no sign of man's response to it, no indication of any power flowing from it. The only result was mockery and railing.

Moreover he was the utter victim of it. The ignominy of the crucifixion allowed no possibility for the expression of noble or dramatic triumph of spirit. Instead it drained his forces and wracked his body and made of him a repulsive, bloody, fly-infested, filthy figure, stretched helplessly on a crossbeam in agony.

There was nothing in his plight to suggest the role of victor. Torment had stripped his body of all dignity and at last thirst overcame him and forced a cry for water from his parched lips.

Reduced to such physical and spiritual agony, his heart must have cried out within him for some word of heavenly comfort, some word of vindication, some sign of confirmation of God's power. And yet, strangely enough no word of encouragement or love came to his stricken heart. The heavens were dumb. The Father, who had spoken so decisively at his baptism and again at the transfiguration, upon whom he had counted and to whom he had given all, now left him alone facing a doubtful destiny, looking stark into the face of evil, unprotected, unconsoled and unsupported. Utterly forsaken, he was alone to face the final soul-assailing doubt that tore at his heart and denied the very validity of the love to which he clung so tenaciously. Alone, he was forced to face not only the possibility of failure but the threat of despair that declares that finally and ultimately such sacrifice is futile; that there is no triumph for goodness, no final ground for trust, no final victory for love; that love, after all, is a helpless orphan in a careless and heartless world. No human soul has ever suffered as Christ must have suffered then.

But had he not suffered that, that cross would have had no triumph in it. For after all, that is the crisis, the test, the crux of faith in love's power, that in a world of hate and cruelty and cynicism, love could survive and triumph of its own self; that alone in the world it should refuse to give up, find faith in its own very essence, clinging despite all to a God of love where there seemed to be no love—and then that it should awaken to find itself at one with the eternal God Himself.

That is the ultimate triumph of that love: following through to the heart of sacrifice, it finally faced the world alone without even God's help, confronted by doubt which is always more terrible than fear because it fathers fear. It faced the world of evil that denies love's validity, derides its power, and impales it on a cross for all to see its impotence —alone and unprotected, bereft of all justification except its own integrity. I say that that complete aloneness, separated from all except evil itself, is the final road that love must tread to triumph.

Evil can force its way and impose its power, can bludgeon and strike and carve its way with cruelty and cry and rail and hurl its torment. Evil has a thousand weapons; love has but one: to suffer and to love despite all. In face of all, unprotected and alone, but still loving. Thus only can love pay the final price and vindicate itself for what it is: the essence of the heart of God Himself.

God does not fall back upon power to triumph. He is His own justification. And that is why, in Christ, He thrust His love into the world, incarnate in man's being, to suffer evil and to meet it finally alone, to suffer His love to bear "the slings and arrows" of a truly outrageous fortune, to suffer evil's most terrible infliction, and so to vindicate the power of love and prove forever that love is stronger than hate, that goodness is stronger than evil, that sacrifice does triumph.

And so I think that at the crucifixion, God restrained His power to interfere and left His love in Christ to stand alone. Love was to be on its own in Christ and so face evil of itself. And it did. It met evil's onslaught and defied doubt, and clung to its own goodness and its own power, and held out despite death's threats, and triumphed gloriously, as Easter testifies.

And I believe that this lonely moment was the climax of God's work in Christ, for Christ was God Himself alone upon that cross, bereft of the power of His might, facing evil's worst, yet uncapitulating and undefeated.

And because of the triumph of that love which gave itself upon the cross and did not give up, our hearts can give themselves to him who trusted himself to that love, who faced death for us and proved the victory of love and so of God Himself, and made himself forever our support, our strength and our redemption, and our final salvation from our guilt and evil's grasp.

THE FIFTH WORD

"I thirst."   *John 19:28*

WE COME NOW to the Fifth Word, "I thirst."—the only word from the cross which refers to Jesus' physical suffering.

It stands alone and yet how perfectly this passage fits the scene and how necessary to complete the story.

Those who have seen wounded men on the battlefield know how awful is the agony of thirst that the wounded suffer. It is no ordinary thirst but one that consumes the whole being of the sufferer with an intolerable craving for water.

Such was the case with Jesus. No part of his body was free from pain. His brow throbbed under the pressure of the cruel crown of thorns which sent little streams of blood trickling down his face. His back burned and ached from the purple welts which the lash had made. His shoulders were raw with the bruises from the weight of the rough-hewn cross he had to carry. The unnatural sag of his unsupported body racked his frame, and when he sought relief for his aching muscles the movement tore the flesh around his nail holes and forced the blood to flow anew from the tender, swollen, festering wounds in his hands and feet. Even his breathing was painful and the air was heavy with the fetid, nauseating odor of dripping blood and running sores.

As time wore on, the heat of noonday, the loss of blood, and the mounting fever all culminated in this terrible thirst. Jesus' thirst was real or he would not have given vent to this cry, for he was not one to seek pity or sympathy. Earlier, at the beginning, he had refused to temper his suffering by accepting the potion of wine mixed with myrrh which the measured mercy of Roman justice allowed to those who were undergoing this cruel form of death. Now this cry for a drink is wrung from his lips.

I have been greatly surprised in my study of this passage to see how many exegetes attempt to explain it away, almost as the Gnostics did, saying that it means that he thirsted for God or that he thirsted for human souls, as though it were not physical thirst he suffered but only spiritual thirst.

To be sure it was spiritual thirst but only because it was the real anguish of bodily thirst that he suffered. The source of his cry was his humanity. It was his oneness with man that drew forth these words, "I thirst," because his body was a man's body. Just as it was also his oneness with man, as well as with God, that drew forth his cry, "Father, forgive them for they know not what they do." He knew their weakness because he was a man himself. They were flesh of his flesh. His lot was man's lot. He never sought to escape it. He never let his unity with God set him apart from his fellow-men. He did not seek to be immune from their sufferings; instead he shared them.

There is a moving scene in Rostand's famous play *L'Aiglon* which may give us a clue to this. You remember that when his bodyguard, the loyal Flambeau, was mortally stricken trying to effect the little Duke's escape from Vienna, the Aiglon, moved by compassion, took him in his arms and tried to comfort his dying moments by transporting him in imagination to the battle of Wagram in which he had taken part, describing the battle and the Emperor's victory, and how Flambeau was carried away by the vivid picture; and then how the anguish of his suffering broke in upon the picture and made him cry out, almost involuntarily *"À boire, à boire!"* "A drink, a drink!"—"I thirst, I thirst!" But even then their imaginations were so carried away by the scene they had evoked, that as he cried there came to them the echo from a thousand anguished throats upon the field of Wagram, *"À boire, à boire, à boire!"*

And then it was that the Aiglon saw that the cry *"À boire!"* wrung from the lips of Flambeau in his agony was part and parcel of the cry of all the wounded lying on the field of Wagram; that history was made up not only of triumph but of suffering and anguish, and above all oneness in the suffering of all mankind. And he understood for the first time that the triumph of Wagram was not all glory but that it was shot through with agony too and that in it men found themselves sharing the common cup of anguish which sinful humanity was heir to through the ages.

Even Jesus didn't try to escape this. Rather in a sense he seems to have embraced it, to prove that his humanity was knit with all humanity.

As one reads the record one finds abundant evidence that in his Passion Jesus felt that he took upon himself the common lot of all men. He accepted the cross, not only because he felt it was God's will, and not only because for love there could be no other way to endure it, but also because in some way he felt that he must take unto himself all of humanity, with its sins and follies and all its consequent suffering; that he must stand in their stead—not before an angry and offended God who demanded a perfect sacrifice to acquit justice, but to share the full measure of the evil that man's plight involved.

It seems to me that the great heresy of the church in our day is not that we do not accept Jesus' deity—we have innumerable dogmas to safeguard that. The great heresy is that we so easily, so carelessly, and so superficially accept his being human. We accept him as a man but not as Man. We set him apart. We feel that as Son of God he is, ipso facto, immune from all the frailties and doubts and temptations that man is harassed by, a sort of superman, not a true son-of-man as he claimed to be. We even go so far as to make him something other than ourselves and so increase the breach between ourselves and him to protect ourselves from any obligation to be like him. We emphasize his Divine Sonship and denaturalize his humanity. And in our worship of him, which he never sought, we lose touch with him and his oneness with us which can save us.

In the French film *Dieu a besoin des Hommes,* which

created so much interest a few years ago, there was a scene in which the sacristan and erstwhile spiritual leader of that priest-forsaken island off the cost of Britanny takes it upon himself to preach a sermon to the Breton fishermen who have pretty much forgotten what religion is all about. Their priest had left them because they had become so hard-hearted, but this indomitable peasant, played by Pierre Fresnay, undertakes to bring them back to God. And he chooses for his text the creed which reads: "I believe in one Lord, Jesus Christ, begotten of his father before all worlds, begotten not made . . . who for us men and for our salvation . . . was made man," and he tells them that it is most important that they remember the creed and particularly that part which says "He was made man"—that God knows what it is to be a man because he accepted our full humanity and became one of us. And in his rude, naive peasant way, he goes on to insist that it is something we ought never to forget, that Jesus was a man like us. That when God sought our salvation He sought it through a man, not an angel or a seraph, but through one who belongs to us, who prized his humanity and carried it even up to and through the cross.

That, I think, is what this cry "I thirst!" confirms, that he was man even unto the end and that he is always one of us, which gives point to Paul's insistence that we have an advocate within the heart of God.

So this word from the cross is very precious; it declares that in him love had to suffer as man suffers. Only thus could he save us, not as God from without, but as man, God's man; that he who would save mankind must identify himself with mankind and suffer with mankind and for mankind.

Leslie Weatherhead, in *The Transforming Friendship,*

quotes an old allegory which recounts a scene at a conclave in Heaven.

An Angel drew near to the Throne of Grace, and God, seeing that he sought something, asked, "What wouldst thou?" And the Angel said, "I would fain be a saviour of men." For the cry of their misery and pain and sin had sounded even in Heaven. "Suffer me to fly down from above and to rescue them." And the host of heaven drew near to listen. And God said, and His voice was very gentle: "Thou wouldst be a saviour of men and yet thine eye is bright and happy and thy heart beats with joy that has never been dimmed. And thy hands are white and clean. Hast thou not beheld my Son?"

And the Angel kept silence, for he was a very new Angel and he understood not these things.

And God said: "Go for a season and dwell with men and see what thou shalt see upon the earth." And the Angel departed.

Now a long time afterward, there stood one before the Throne and his mien was sad, yet from his presence there shone a great hope and a great joy. And God said: "Who art thou?" and he said: "I am that Angel whom Thou didst send to dwell awhile with men." And God said: "But thine eye is dim with pain and thy heart is broken and thy hands are stained with blood."

And the Angel answered: "I have seen sorrow and pain and sin. The sons of men grind one another for wealth, and spill their brothers' blood for power, and trample their sisters that they may know pleasure; and when I saw, my eyes were dimmed, and when I loved, my heart was broken, and when I strove to lift the fallen, my hands were stained with blood." And God said, to try him: "And thou hast returned that thy wounds may be healed." And the Angel said: "No, Lord, for man's sake I would cling to my pain. How else could I save him? Bid me return, I pray Thee, to the place of man's anguish for I cannot raise him save as I stand and suffer at his side."

And as he spoke there was a movement in Heaven and all the hosts thereof turned and looked and behold! a lamb standing as though it had been newly slain.

And God turned to the Angel and said: "Go! For thou too hast learned to be a saviour of men."

Perhaps it is true that this thirst on the cross was born of his thirst for men's souls, after all.

THE SIXTH WORD

"It is finished."   *John 19:30*

No DOUBT the devastating torrid heat of noonday and the mounting agony of his wounds had taken their toll of his waning strength and had left Jesus with an increasing sense of the imminent nearness of death. His power to endure more or to respond or resist further was exhausted, and this certainty of death's momentary approach brought to his lips this parting cry, "It is finished!" We don't know whether it was a cry of victory, "It is finished!" in crescendo, or a cry of relinquishment, "It is finished." We are not sure just what he meant was finished. It may have been his agony, his ordeal, his testing; it may have been his life, his work, his mission, his destiny. There are many possibilities.

But one thing which these words quite probably meant was that it was all over, that life had come to its end, that there was nothing more that he could do. It was finished. The long and often painful path of obedience which he had followed so loyally, and sometimes blindly, had come to its termination.

The demands of his Father, who spoke within his heart, had brought him irrevocably to the cross and death. And now it was all over. No miracle had intervened to vindicate or save him. For good or ill, life was now out of his hands. Had he wished to do more or to say more, he could not have. His earthly days had reached their end. Nothing more could be added. There is an irrevocable finality about these words, "It is finished!" And in this he was like all of us, for the day will come for each one of us when we too must say: "It is over." There will be no more that we can do on earth, no further opportunity to change our course, to make amends, to right what is wrong or to repair our mistakes.

They will have to stand as they are. It will all be over. The encouraging word can no longer be said, the word of forgiveness can no longer be spoken, the act of kindness can no longer be performed, the declaration of loyalty no longer be made, nor the gesture of love. Life's opportunity will be over.

This is a sobering fact.

Do you remember the scene in Thornton Wilder's play *Our Town,* in which Emily, who had died in childbirth, was given the opportunity to return to Grover's Corners to relive her twelfth birthday, and how disillusioning the realization of her lost opportunity was and how irrevocable was death?

It is a touching scene. She went back but the experience as seen from the other side was not a very satisfactory one. Everyone—her brothers and sisters and even her father and mother—was too preoccupied with busyness about living to stop even to see the others or ever really to get what life had to give. Once, in the midst of things, Emily stopped to plead: "Oh, Mama, just look at me one minute as though you really saw me. . . . Just for a moment now we're all together— Mama, just for a moment let's be happy— Let's look at one another!"

But life went on, preoccupied and fleeting, and at last Emily cried out to the Stage Manager: "I can't! I can't go on! Oh, oh, it goes so fast! We don't have time to look at one another. . . . I didn't *realize!* So all that was going on and we never noticed!"

And so at last she asked to be taken back, but before she left she turned to say goodbye with these words; no one who has ever heard them will forget the pathos of them:

"Take me back. . . . But first, wait! One more look! Goodbye! Goodbye, world! Goodbye, Grover's Corners!— Mama and Papa! Goodbye to clocks ticking! . . . and Mama's sunflowers—and food and coffee—and new-ironed dresses and hot baths—and sleeping and waking up!— Oh, earth, you're too wonderful for anyone to realize you!"

And then she turns to the Stage Manager:

"Do any human beings ever realize life while they live it—every, every minute?"

"No," he answers. "Saints and poets maybe—they do some."

There you have it, that's why we find it hard to face the finality of the end of life here. We haven't made the most of it. We let it slip through our fingers without making anything of it, anything worth while. It's God's gift to us but we mutilate it.

But not so with Christ. He could not only accept the fact that it was over but he could also say that it was completed. It was finished! He had fulfilled his mission. He had done what it had been laid upon him to do. He had been loyal to the end and had fulfilled the purpose of his life. He had no sense of having fallen short. There is no indication of regret.

He had drunk the cup that God had proffered him to its last bitter dregs. He could say, as no other, "It is finished," and mean not only that it was over but also that it was completed.

If he shared with us the fact that life's opportunity must come to an end, he differed from us in that he had fulfilled his opportunity.

Who of us can say that he has completed his life? Who of us can say that he has met the day's requirement and filled it full? We all of us know that there is much we have done which should have been left undone and much we have failed to do that we should have done. Our prayer of confession confesses our inadequacy. Had we sinned in nothing more, we should still have to face the fact that none of us has made the most of the opportunity that life has given to us. We shall all pass from this world with uncompleted lives no matter what the tally of our years.

Not so with Christ. He lived but a few years more than three decades but he faced death with no plea for more time or more opportunity. There was no haunting sense of personal failure or inadequacy, no intimation of the cry that came from the lips of the dying Cecil Rhodes, "So little done, so much to do!" He had not failed his calling or betrayed his vision.

As the writer of the Fifty-third Chapter of Isaiah intimated in that great prophetic passage so admirably fitted to his life, "He saw the travail of his soul and was satisfied with it." He had done the work that he felt he had been appointed to do and he found satisfaction in it even while he hung in agony on the cross. And so in a sense this cry was also a declaration of victory.

Even the cross had not forced his capitulation to evil.

Love had been loyal to the finish. No temptation had been strong enough to make him yield to it. He had come to the end, the bitterest of all ends, without giving way to evil's subtleties. He had not capitulated to the appeal for power or for wordly vindication; nor to compromise or retaliation. He had remained true to the very end, despite the terrible pressure put on him by the events that had brought him to the cross; despite his disciples' cowardice, despite Caiaphas' malice and Herod's wiles and Pilate's temporizing; despite the mob's unreasoned hatred and the Roman soldiers' callous cruelty, and the crowd's curious indifference and the cross's torture.

Despite all this mounting tide of evil that threatened to engulf his loyalty to a good God, born of love, he never betrayed it even though it brought suffering with it. He finished his mission without denying the love that had sent him on it. He completed its obligation with unbroken fidelity to the Spirit that fathered him.

He saw the travail of his soul and found it satisfied.

But this cry has become more than a declaration of his own action. It is also a declaration to all mankind that God's work in him was done, that divine love's encounter with evil had been consummated with victory at the very point where evil had been left free to do its worst. And that in that process the impotence of evil to overcome goodness and love had been proved beyond question of a doubt. Evil had done its worst and had failed miserably. The last rampart of evil's stronghold had been taken, the strife was over, the victory won. Love and faith were still alive within him. They had triumphed.

The cosmic conflict had been resolved at the crucial point, the point where love had suffered all that evil could impose, all the forces that evil could rally in human heart and hand, in both state and ecclesiastical authority, in the powers

of darkness, and wickedness in high places. Even there evil
had failed. He had proved its vulnerability. Henceforth men
could face evil, convinced that victory was sure, that the
issue did not hang in the balance.

Recently a noted journalist-publisher told us of his
conversation with Whittaker Chambers in which the latter
said that, despite the fact that he had broken with Communism and had cast his lot with the side which he honestly
felt was right, nevertheless he was convinced that it was the
losing side.

Not so the Christian. Ever since love's victory on the
Cross of Christ, man has known that the battle has been
won. The outcome is sure. We struggle, not in darkness
lighted only by the flickering lamp of stoic hope, but in the
full light of the Gospel of sure victory in Christ, confident—
as St. Paul said—that nothing, absolutely nothing is strong
enough to separate us from the love of God in Christ.

At heart it is finished. The cosmic struggle is over.
Henceforth evil, for all its seeming power in high and low
places, for all the forces both material and spiritual that it
would lay its hands on in our world, is fighting a losing
battle. Christ has won the struggle on evil's home territory.
The Prince of Darkness has been proven vanquished.

What we need is not more desperate determination to
fight, but more confident faith in our Lord and his weapons,
for wherever and whenever we share his spirit, we also share
his victory, which is not only ultimate but also absolute.

It is finished! The victory is his.

THE SEVENTH WORD

"Father, into thy hands I commend my spirit."
Luke 23:46

From one standpoint this might quite reasonably be the last desperate cry of a broken, defeated, dying spirit, giving up his dream.

From another it might be the final triumphant declaration of a confident faith putting his complete loyalty into the hands of the Father.

There is a vast difference between them but, in either case, it is a poignant utterance. Because we see it in the light of subsequent events, I think we are inclined to misinterpret it and miss its deeper meaning. The fact is that we see Jesus' experience in the light of what happened later and tend to read triumph and certainty into it and to interpret it to fit our thought of him as we know him now.

Of course, if you think of Jesus as some kind of a special peculiar person who never knew the pangs of doubt and was never tempted, "like as we are," who knew from the beginning just what he was to go through so that the cross was a kind of play-acting of something known from the start, with some real physical suffering to be sure, and some kind of mystical suffering also, but no real agony of mind and spirit as we know it—then these words have no poignancy in them.

But if he was emptied of all this and, like us, could know temptation as the Bible says he did, and if his heart could be assailed by doubt as the record indicates, however much he put it away, and if he could face the possibility of defeat in the cross, then these words, following on the words in the Garden of Gethsemane, become for us the final, hard-won triumph of his hard-pressed faith in God.

If he never had to face doubt as we know it or be tempted as we are at the deeper levels, then he never could share our life at its deeper levels. But this is what he did, and at the deepest possible level. Jesus faced what we have to face if we would have faith in God, but he went on where we hold back; he put his faith in love and God to the ultimate test and faced things where the crisis was most crucial, where everything was at stake.

He put his life into the hands of God unconditionally and let Him take him right through to the place where faith had to face the ultimate trial. And it wasn't easy and it wasn't play-acting.

He answered evil's ultimatum in a cross and met it with unflinching love. He gave to God a completely loyal instrument with which to do for us what he had not been able to do before, but it wasn't an automatic process untouched by doubt and the temptation to abandon it. Indeed the greater his dedication to God's will, the greater the conflict within him and the more terrible the battle he had to fight with evil and doubt, facing that cross.

And mind you, this was no ordinary cross. Something was happening there that had never happened before but Jesus was not dead sure of it. He was pitting his faith and love against the power of the cross to break them, and it was a terrifying experience that centered there. You may be sure it involved a soul-testing inner battle, for if it didn't, the spiritual experience neither of Gethsemane nor of the cross had any reality.

There is some evidence in the record that Jesus himself

did not expect things as they finally worked out. I don't think
he knew exactly what would happen or how it would happen.
His was too great a destiny for his humanity to comprehend.
All he knew was that he must remain loyal to the will of
the Father as the Father revealed it to him and to take the
consequences and leave the dénouement to God. But he did
expect vindication, and that is where doubt tried to get at
him. Doubt at this crucial level is far more terrible to suffer
than any physical suffering, especially for one who loved men
and wanted their redemption as much as Jesus did. And the
thought that maybe he was all wrong, as Peter had suggested, to risk a cross, that maybe he would not be vindicated
and love not triumph over evil but become its victim, was a
fearful thought. You see, love had to face the cross as a
risk. And that is what gives meaning to these words of
Jesus from the cross. They are part of a sequence: First, the
temptation to abandon it,

"Father, let this cup pass from me."

And then the response,

"Not my will but thine be done,"

and then the doubt again,

"My God, my God, why hast thou forsaken me?"

And lastly in the face of final defeat,

"Father, into thy hands I commend my spirit."

Without the triumph of the last, all the others are futile.
That's crucial. Was God in the process or not?

Consider the facts. Here was a man who had given
himself over to utter obedience to the will of the Father,
come what might. If a cross was the direction in which love

called him, he would take it; he would not fail the Father. And so he set his feet upon the Via Dolorosa.

And what was the result? Opening skies? A legion of angels? Triumph and vindication? The Kingdom come with power and glory? The conversion of the onlookers? A great victory?

Not at all! It was cruel suffering and scorn and ridicule and pity; raw, burning welts upon his back where he had been flogged, throbbing pain about his brow where the crown of thorns had been mercilessly pressed, swelling wounds where the nails pierced his hands and feet, thirst and dejection.

Instead of love's triumph, evil was doing its worst to wring the last red drop of suffering from his soul, trying by every cruel means to break and crush his loyalty to the love that was within him. Pain racked his body. The agonizing weight of it as it hung there tore at his tender, festering wounds until at last his ebbing resistance confirmed the desperate reality of the defeat that evil had wrought upon him, the final certainty of his impending death.

That is the awful sequel to that hour in the garden. Seen in its stark reality, this innocent man hanging dying upon a cross, despite the love which he had shed so richly on the world, has no reasonableness about it. If that is where following the will of God ends, it is utterly idiotic. Yes, it is more, it is blasphemously heartless.

You see, the devastating defeat of the cross makes this question of loyalty to the will of God crucial. It's all very well to talk about the power of sacrificial love but over and over again love is checkmated and thwarted and frustrated, ending upon a cross. Over and over again! That's why practical people don't take it seriously. Too often it doesn't work.

Let's face it. This business of Christian discipleship is not a matter of finding a road to success or happiness or felicitous living. It is the way of suffering love and it has a cross at its heart. It calls upon us to deny ourselves and take up a cross and follow in the path of sacrificial love, and to accept the suffering that it may bring to us.

Christianity, no matter how many pious phrases we put upon our stamps or on our coins, is not a formula for successful achievement, least of all a way to be respectable and admirable. Lived as Christ lived it, it pushes faith right up against a wall and sets up a cross, and demands that we take the consequences of love and either commit ourselves to the Father's hands or acknowledge frankly that it doesn't make sense in this hard, evil world of ours.

There is no use trying to fool ourselves into thinking that Christian discipleship—following the Sermon on the Mount and the twelfth chapter of Romans and the thirteenth of First Corinthians, renouncing one's self and giving one's self to sacrificial love, no matter what the circumstances—is one which is practical and reasonable.

Christian love may never see its effective fulfillment. The one we love may never respond to it, may never change his ways, may instead become more bitter, may continue to hate and malign. Instead of being requited, love may be repulsed or crucified. It may all end in rejection and defeat, the victim of animosity, calumny and even cruelty; but it must never cease to be love and it must never seek to evade the suffering involved. It must go on committing itself in obedience to the Father and His way, and trusting His inscrutable purposes. Only thus can it find its fulfillment.

It isn't a practical way or an effective way calculated to sweep all before it. It may end in a cross. It may be torn apart and bled white and left to die, as Jesus was left to die at Calvary.

Often enough it will seem like utter foolishness and utter failure, but the only answer is to say as Jesus did, not in desperation but in confident faith, "Father, into thy hands I commit it all." Into Thy hands!

Seen from any other point of view, Jesus' sacrifice is pure folly; a good man, lured on by loyalty and love, destroyed on a criminal's gibbet; pure foolishness, unless there is One into whose hands he can commit his spirit and his work, Who can make something of them.

That's the alternative. Either he can commit his spirit into the hands of the One whose will he has accepted and have it perfected, or he will go down in betrayal and defeat into the oblivion of an utterly foolish experiment in selfless sacrifice and betrayed love. And so with us. Either like his Master, the Christian believes that the hands of God are there to receive him and to fulfill his loyalty, or there is no rhyme or reason in that loyalty. Certainly in a sin-ridden, evil world, it may end upon a cross.

This is the crux of the whole matter of discipleship. Our faith demands that we believe that love is not an orphan in a heartless universe that mangles and crushes it and throws it aside on the refuse heap, but is of the very essence of God's own Spirit; that the goodness impaled on a cross of suffering can still commit itself to the Spirit that wooed it and lured it on, and trust itself to Him, confident that He can gather it to Himself and use it for His purposes, obscure to us though they may be.

That is faith's necessary sequence. Once having submitted oneself to the Father's will, one must commit oneself to the Father's hands. Obedience has no meaning unless it be sustained by One to whom in confidence we can commit our lives, with all their broken, fragmentary efforts for good. Often we cannot see what good it will do. Often when we are loyal to Christ's way it means only defeat and frustration. Often we are tempted to forsake the Christian way and to fall back upon the expedient way whose results we can see.

Often the Christian way is dark, its meaning obscure, its suffering bitter, and we are tempted to cry out, "My God, my God, why hast thou forsaken me?"

But that, my friends, is because we are not willing to trust our lives and our work to God's hands, as Jesus did. We want to see love's consummation now, its victory now. We are not willing to let loyalty and suffering have their perfect work in His hands. We want to shape them to success ourselves, when the real and only answer is, "Commit yourselves and your efforts and your destiny and your suffering into the Father's hands for His perfecting."

His ways are not our ways but His ways are the ways of love and they are sure. His purposes are beyond our understanding but He can use our defeat and suffering for the fulfilling of His rich purposes in ways which we cannot see from the midst of our suffering, if only we will commit ourselves into His hands.

That is where our faith must finally bring us, to the side of Christ, for at heart Christian discipleship calls for an adventure in love which accepts suffering and even frustration and commits it to God's hands, confident that He has the answer and the power to use it and fulfill it.

And the highest final act of faith of the Christian is to say, as did the Master, "Father, not my will but thine be done, for into thy hands I commit my life, with all its broken purposes, its suffering and its defeats, to be used and perfected by thee."

THE IMPACT OF THE CROSS

And when they had come to the place which is called
The Skull, there they crucified him.   Luke 23:33

W<small>E LIVE SO FAR</small> from the cross that it is hard for us to see it for what it was. Certainly it was nothing like the burnished crosses which we put in our chancels. How much more appropriate it would be if we had a rough-hewn, blood-stained, wooden cross above that table, and if we must have a picture, to have men of our own day about it, farmhands and fisher-folk, steel puddlers and sharecroppers, clerks and taxi-drivers, and preachers and priests, and businessmen and engineers and soldiers. For we all had a hand in it. The cross unhappily seems so far off and so unreal when really what it is and what it does is so contemporary. The people about it were people like us.

Let us look back for a moment at that first cross on Calvary's hill. Strange thing about that cross, how differently it affected people. Some wept over it. Some sneered at it. Some found solace in it. Some wondered at it. Some gloated over it. Some despaired in it. Some ignored it because they were hardened to it. Some exulted in it because their spirits were spiteful. Some were crushed by it because their hopes seemed destroyed on it. Some were struck by it because they had never seen a man die like this man. One cross, many consequences!

And herein is a parable of life. We are ruined or re-deemed by life's circumstances, or rather by our reaction to life's circumstance. A cross may lift us up or hasten us down toward perdition. It may be a means of grace or a means of damnation. The word of God in the cross of Christ may be an opportunity or a judgment. It all depends upon our capacity to react to it whether it speaks to our condition or not. Two men may see and respond to the same experience, but for one it may mean a new vision of life and for the other a mere commonplace unheeded and unrecognized. One may be better for it and the other will surely be the worse, for what does not make one better always makes one worse.

So with those who came in contact with that cross. It was a two-edged sword which cut not only at the man who hung upon it but at all those around it. When evil has its way no man escapes its touch for good or ill. There was Pilate, for instance. He ordered it against his will to be sure, but he ordered it none the less. He resented it. It put him on the spot in a way that he hated. It haunted his soul with indecision until at last he was forced to make a decision that he would have given anything in the world to have escaped. It left him perplexed and confused and regretful. It showed up the shallowness of his ideal of justice. It exposed him for the slave of expediency that he was. It revealed the poverty of his courage and the feebleness of his conviction and showed him up for the moral opportunist he really was. It spelled tragedy for him for it turned an opportunity into a tragic failure. For Pilate who might have been known through the ages as the protector of Christ now has his name recorded in history only because he failed him. That is what the cross did to Pilate.

And the cross did something to Peter, Peter the confident. It shocked him the first time he heard of it and when he faced it, it showed him that the human heart, no matter how well-intentioned, can be very weak and very perfidious; that being forewarned is not enough; that lip service does not prevent denial; that one can protest loyalty and spit out expletives with the same breath, repeat creeds and curses with the same tongue; that loyalty has to be disciplined to be deep, and deep to be impregnable. It revealed to poor Peter the weakness of his allegiance and his need of God's grace like the rest of us. The cross left him conscience-stricken and heartsore and humble, but still loyal to his Master—and one day it made him a saint, when he shared it himself!

And then there was Judas Iscariot, Judas the practical, the arranger, the earthly idealist who tried to force the hand of Jesus hoping perhaps that he would declare himself and set up his Kingdom then and there. But it was a failure, for his hopes were false because they were selfish. He wanted the Kingdom to come for what could be had from it, as so many of us use our religion, and he saw all his fond ambitions dashed to pieces on the cross. And so he found himself disillusioned by his ill-placed zeal and left crushed and tortured and guilt-stricken. It was more than he could stand. For him the cross was stark tragedy. It drove hope from his soul and sent him into despair and forever attached to his name the onus that goes only to Quislings and Lavals and those ambitious opportunists who sell out the best in the hope of personal gain, only to find that their greedy desire has betrayed life's opportunity. One cannot, as Jesus himself said, "serve God and mammon," Christ and ambition.

Then there were Annas and Caiaphas, the high priests. The cross did something to them for it let them damn their own souls. It was an evil day for them when the measure of their malice was matched by the measure of their opportunity. That is what the cross gave them. It gave their hatred and their anger a perfect instrument for their most dastardly expression and so they had full rein to damn themselves. And in their attempt to ruin Jesus they ruined themselves. Sometimes it is the mercy of God that we cannot wreak the vengeance that we wish or work the evil that we desire, for it prevents evil's wreaking upon us the vengeance that it most surely would. We can be glad that we do not always have the means for doing what we would lest it become the means for destroying our souls. And so with Annas and Caiaphas. Because they had power in their hands they won their way and they lost their souls. That is what power can do to a man or a nation.

And then there was Simon of Cyrene who suddenly found the cross forced upon his shoulders, the man who was transformed in a moment from a bystander into a participant. The cross did something to him. It put a new and unwelcome burden upon him, it brought him peremptorily face to face with life's imperious demands, it forced him to be a part of something he wanted to avoid. Against his will it made him a party to the crucifixion. That is the way we feel, some of us, about things today, is it not? And yet out of that experience there came to Simon a benediction, for in making him a yoke-fellow of the cross it brought him into companionship with the Captain of men's souls and it drew him and his two sons, Rufus and Alexander, into the fellowship of Christ's King-dom through the fellowship of his suffering, through the doorway of an imposition. The grace of God entered his life through that experience as only the grace of God can.

At the foot of that central cross there was a Roman soldier who stood guard. He had been detailed for the unpleasant duty of executing the crucifixion. I think inside he must have rebelled against it. He accepted his task but he hated it. At least he did not seem to justify it and rationalize it like Simon of Cyrene. I think he too resented the imposition that the cross had brought to him. But like Simon he too found a new vision in that cross for it revealed to him the heroism of love, the glory of sacrifice, the dignity of vicarious suffering and the godlikeness of magnanimity of spirit. And all these things that he saw in Christ cast such a halo about his head that it forced from the lips of the soldier the words of admiration and devotion, "Surely he was a Son of God for only a Son of God could die like that." The cross opened his eyes. A sense of our common guilt can do that if one is sensitive to it. Strange, is it not, that those two who had been strangers to Jesus and who had had the cross thrust into their experience found in it a benediction? They both seemed to have realized their own personal entanglement in the corporate evil of the world and to have seen in Christ something that gave them hope that they could meet it and not be destroyed by it, lost in it.

But there were two others hung there on Calvary's hill, one on the right hand and one on the left, and the cross did something to both of them, for one was damned by the bitterness that it brought to his soul and the other was saved by the hope that it aroused within him. One railed on Christ for his impotence and one blessed him for his compassion. One passed into perdition with cynical curses on his lips and the other stepped into Paradise with a new light in his soul. They suffered together, but the suffering of one thrust him forever from Christ's side and the suffering of the other drew him forever into his presence. And suffering still offers these alternatives to us today.

And then there were Mary and Salome, the women who clung to the cross to the last and then tenderly lifted down its precious burden. The cross did something to them also. It revealed to them, and to all the world since, the depth of their loyalty. It cut their hearts to the quick, it left them wounded and bleeding and heartsick, but it also drew forth the deep devotion that they cherished, and kept them there by his side through all the long and agonizing hours that the sun beat upon his wounds. These women stood by when others forsook him. They stayed by his side through all the shame and scorn and spite. They shared his misery and his humiliation. The cross brought out the best that was in them and their memory is fragrant to this day. The cross came poignantly into their lives too. Love saw them through as love can.

And then there was the crowd of onlookers, the curious, the pitiful, the sneering, and the indifferent. The cross did something to them that they did not know, for it judged them for their blindness and their carelessness and their apathy and their callousness. They neither protested nor took his part. They passed him by, and the cross condemns them for their careless unconcern. One day they shall know what they missed on that day at Calvary. We are damned by what we fail to see and do, as much as by what we do. We are damned by our blindness and our deafness, as Jesus said. When we are sure we are right and safe, when humility and poverty of spirit find no room in our life, then beware, we may be missing divine destiny.

And then last, the cross did something to the heart of God, for it gave God an instrument to show to the world what love could and would do to save us. It cleared the issue and struck at the heart of things. It drove the powers of evil to their last rampart and then vanquished them and gave God the victory. For Christ, His Son, made himself God's point of fire coming into our life and drawing unto himself the evil of the world. In him God suffered the outrages of sin and in him He triumphed over evil and brought redemption to the world for you and for me.

And the question we must face is: What will the cross do to our life? What will we see in it? What will it make us do? Will it make us say, humbly and contritely and hopefully with a deep gratitude in our hearts:

Beneath the cross of Jesus I fain would take my stand,
The Shadow of a mighty rock within a weary land;

A home within the wilderness, a rest upon the way,
From the burning of the noon-tide heat, and the burden
of the day.

Upon that cross of Jesus mine eyes at times can see
The very dying form of One who suffered there for me;
And from my smitten heart with tears two wonders I
confess,—
The wonders of His glorious love and my unworthiness.

I take, O cross, thy shadow for my abiding place;
I ask no other sunshine than the sunshine of His face;
Content to let the world go by, to know no gain nor loss,
My sinful self my only shame, my glory all the cross.

ELIZABETH C. CLEPHANE

✤ ✤ ✤ *Easter*

THE EASTER MANIFESTO

"Ye seek Jesus of Nazareth, which was crucified; he is risen; he is not here."   Mark 16:6

No OTHER WORDS have meant as much to human history as these three simple words, "He is risen!" Today, two thousand years later, they re-echo around the world on the lips of Christians everywhere. Let us contemplate the significance of this Easter greeting, taking each word in turn, beginning with the verb.

The verb *is* is used for the statement of a fact. And the first point is that the risen Christ is not a conjecture or a supposition or a hope, but a reality. "He *is* risen."

It is high time, as Dr. George Buttrick has suggested, that our Easter thinking should be lifted from the subjunctive or conditional mood of "If Christ be risen" into the indicative affirmative mood of "Now *is* Christ risen from the dead." For the resurrection is one of the best attested facts of history.

For one thing, the record itself is trustworthy; it will stand scrutiny. All the signs of an authentic narrative are to be found in those simple Gospel accounts—the absence of labored proof, the characteristic variation in detail, and the essential agreement in important facts. If the various records were absolutely consistent we should have reason to doubt them but the Gospel records are like witnesses in a crowd. One says, "It was like this"; another says, "No, like this"; and still another says, "No, not at all; it was rather like this" —all giving unconscious testimony that the fact is greater than their capacity to describe or explain it. It is generally conceded in courts of law that when witnesses differ in details but agree substantially on the main points, the principal event actually took place.

These accounts are clearly not fictions. The record bears the stamp of authenticity. It is too audacious for invention and too candid for fabrication; it is written with the artless carelessness of truthfulness, without any labored attempt to marshal proof. Indeed the vital evidence appears almost a casual statement. The Evangelists write with conviction and confidence but not with argument, as though they were so sure of the reality of their story that to build up a case was unnecessary. There is every evidence here of the impact of an amazing, overwhelming experience which astounded them.

Moreover, on what other basis than that of the reality of the resurrection could one account for the remarkable change that took place in the outlook and spirit of those disciples following Easter? It is true that the early Church was born at Pentecost, but Pentecost would not have existed if there had been no Easter. Easter was transforming! Remember, Jesus was put to death upon a despised Roman cross, a criminal's gibbet, which for a Messiah was absolutely unthinkable. It was contrary to all reason, and an affront to propriety. On the face of it, seen from their standpoint, there could be no divine providence in such a miserable, disgraceful extinction.

And it is also unreasonable to think that the resurrection was the natural consummation of their desire and hope. Hope died in confusion on Good Friday. The disciples had no thought that Jesus was going to rise from the tomb as he did or they most certainly would have stayed around the tomb to see it occur. They would at least have had a lookout posted and they would have been ready for it.

And certainly belief in the resurrection was not the inevitable reaction that might be expected to follow grief. The fact is they had to be convinced almost against their better judgment. The record quite frankly states that at first the disciples were skeptical about the news of the resurrection. The empty tomb was a source of bewilderment for them and there were those who simply could not believe the appearances.

Friday was a day of tragedy and grief; Saturday was a day of disappointed hopes and despair; but Easter became a day of joy and of renewed hope and faith, faith on which the Church was built. Now can one explain that if not by a genuine resurrection?

But what is more, Jesus did not die and become a cherished memory, a loved and mourned departed friend. He arose and became a spiritual presence, a companion and leader. There is not, in all the record, with the possible exception of that on the way to Emmaus, a single word of regret at his passing, or a single memorial raised to his memory. The only memorial that survived is a memorial meal which has become a means of renewing loyalty to a living Lord.

Paul was quite right in making the resurrection the essential basis for the Gospel. There would have been no Gospel but for the *fact* of the resurrection.

One could go on with other evidence—the grave wraps lying on the sepulcher ledge just as they had collapsed, a fact which was very convincing to those who came to the tomb as they reflected on it; the utter impossibility of any of his followers having stolen away the body—their consciences would never have permitted them to keep it a secret; and the certainty that the authorities, who hated the Christians, would have routed out the facts and used them effectively against them. And last of all, no person wounded as Jesus was could have hung for over three hours on the cross and then have had the power to extricate himself from the grave clothes weighted down with burial spices, or to escape, even if he had not been dead when he was taken down from the cross. Had there been the slightest doubt of this, it would have haunted the hearts of his followers and cut the nerve of their gospel.

All the evidence points to the fact of the resurrection. It may be too appalling for our hearts to accept but it is not too unreasonable for our minds if we are honest.

But facts are not as effective in men's lives as are the implications they involve. And these words, "He is risen," are more significant because of the *One* to whom they refer than because of the *fact* to which they refer. *"He* is risen." Jesus Christ is risen!

There had been many stories of resuscitations and spirit appearances before. Ancient history is full of them. But such appearances had had little effect on religious faith. The real significance of Easter lay not in the fact that One had been raised from the dead but that *Jesus* had been raised from the dead.

Suppose some indifferent person had risen, just somebody down the street. That fact would never have made an Easter. No one would have attached the slightest importance to such an event except as a wonder to marvel at. The significance of the risen Christ did not lie in its corroboration of immortality. That was not the central fact. The central fact lay in the fact that it was Jesus, the One who had taught forgiveness and love and good will, the One who had trusted his very life to love and had given it on a cross, it was *he* who had risen again. "Fear not," said the shining one at the tomb, "Ye seek Jesus, the One who was crucified. He is risen." The One who was crucified was risen.

Have you ever thought that of all the crosses in Palestine, and there had been thousands of crosses, literally thousands of crucifixions there, his was the only one that stood out, the only one that is remembered, the only one that has any significance for us? It is true that there were two others on crosses who have come down in history, but they are remembered only because they hung by his side.

That cross was significant because of him who hung upon it, and that tomb was significant because it was he who had hung on that cross who rose from it. The cross and the resurrection belong together. Jesus made immortality specific, for the cross indicates the kind of life that is on the "other side." It is the clue to heaven.

Jesus Christ, not Mohammed; Jesus Christ, not Napoleon; Jesus Christ, not Socrates, rose from the dead; and it was not wisdom that was justified on that Easter morn, but sacrifice and love. The One who trusted to love even though he was crucified, the One who had been on the cross, was the One who had risen.

It makes a great difference, that cross. It makes immortality serious, for on that cross Jesus flung his earnestness about sin against man's carelessness, his love against sin's power, his faith against man's doubt, his forgiveness against sin's reality, his sacrifice against evil's ruthlessness. That cross made immortality very specific, very definite.

We have tended to water down our thought about immortality until it has become a sort of vague confidence that everything will work out all right in the end, that it does not make much difference what one does or what one believes or how one lives or to what one gives one's allegiance; everything will be ironed out "over there." God is too good to damn us.

Well, God is good, more than we have any idea. But He let Jesus go to a cross, and that cross takes all the casualness from immortality. There is nothing in the Gospel story or in the whole New Testament that even intimates that the one who is indifferent to the moral and spiritual values that are in Christ will suddenly become fit for immortality. That would make the cross utterly senseless. Jesus brought immortality to light in a special way, and those who share the life and spirit of Christ are the ones who will enter into life. It belongs to the Christlike spirit, the Christ-possessed heart. And one day, somewhere, we must learn that if we are to share the immortality God has intended for us.

And again, those words, "He is risen," are significant because of the triumph they affirm, because they give that life and that cross the backing of the universe. He is RISEN, and in that resurrection his kind of life and spirit are forever vindicated. It proved that his life did not go out; it went on.

There had been a lurking doubt in the minds of some of his followers as to whether he was the Messiah of God. Even John the Baptist had his doubts, you remember. Jesus' way of life appealed to something deep within them; it did them good to hear his words; he drew forth their admiration and affection, but nevertheless his outlook was often so radically different from the one they knew, that sometimes they doubted whether it was anything more than a dream— this loving one's enemies; this humility and selflessness; this giving of one's self in service to the point of sacrifice. That doubt haunted them, and when at last he let the authorities take him and crucify him, it was more than their hearts could stand, or understand. How, in view of his shameful death on the criminal's cross, could it be possible that he should be God's appointed One? How could he be God's Messiah since God had let him down? That terrible cry from the cross, "My God, my God, why hast thou forsaken me?" was evidence of that.

You can see what Easter did to that doubt. The crucial question was not immortality; it was, "Did this man Jesus really have God's word and God's backing, or was he just a cosmic anachronism?" And that question still comes to our hearts at times, does it not? When we face Jesus' way of life and his teaching about life, it is either absolute folly or it is eternal triumph to follow him—one or the other. That is why the resurrection is central to our faith. Christianity is a great adventure. But Easter has confirmed God's vindication of Christ. "Now hath God raised Jesus from the dead, the first fruit of God's purpose." The resurrection put the hallmark of heaven on Jesus' life and cross. During His lifetime Jesus had oriented life in love and goodness and forgiveness and sacrificial living. Easter oriented these in eternity. Easter convinced them that Christ's love had had its origin in God's heart and that Christ's words and way of living were native to God's universe. If they did not fit the world, it was the world that was wrong, not Jesus as they had feared. He had triumphed.

They knew now that Jesus' life was the kind of life that evil and death could not wipe out—they had no power over it. He had not eluded them; he had overcome them. And all who share that quality of life have permanence in them. They too belong to God's eternity through Christ if his love is in them, no matter who they may be.

The coming of Christ had been the hope of Israel. The resurrection made him God's Word for the world. It gave to faith a new dimension. The creator of the world had given him his corroboration. The resurrection lifted Christ out of

the setting of Palestine and made him the universal Christ—
God's Word for all mankind. It carried Christianity beyond
the bounds of race or clan or sect. Christ was not to be followed in narrow sectarian channels or petty partisan ways
but across all barriers. In him, as Paul soon discovered and
declared, there was to be neither Jew nor Gentile, Greek nor
barbarian, Scythian nor Roman, bond nor free, male nor fe-
male. Easter set the Christian faith in a cosmic, universal
setting. Christ was not one of many but the *One* in whom all
men could trust and whose life all men could share.

That is what transformed the disciples and made them
bold, so that they could face the Roman pike and the "lion's
gory mane." The resurrection and the risen Christ gave them
an invincible conviction that the life that was attached to him
was impregnable. He gave them a sense of life's cosmic orien-
tation and cosmic security which made them triumphant
spirits. The risen Christ became their companion, their
Master, and their contemporary Lord, the impact of whose
presence transformed and glorified their lives.

That is the fact by which all Christendom lives—the
Lord of love is not dead. He is alive and by our side, the
Master of our hearts.

> And warm, sweet, tender, even yet
>   A present help is He;
> And faith had still its Olivet
>   And love its Galilee.
>
> The healing of His seamless dress
>   Is by our beds of pain;
> We touch Him in life's throng and press,
>   And we are whole again.

He is risen, and his spirit is forever with us—the triumphant
and the conquering Christ.

THE ROAD TO EMMAUS

"Ought not Christ to have suffered these things, and to enter into his glory?"   Luke 24:26

CERTAINLY this story of the walk to Emmaus is one of the most beautiful and significant incidents in the Gospels. The crucifixion had taken place three days before and as the third day drew toward its close two of the disciples, convinced apparently that nothing more would come of the movement launched by their erstwhile leader, were making their way home to Emmaus to take up their old-time routine.

A cloud of perplexity and disillusionment hung over them. Only a week before, the movement centered in Jesus had been on the crest of a wave of enthusiasm and acclaim, facing what seemed to be a brilliant future. Today its leader was dead, its reputation enshrouded in shame, its collapse complete, and most of its adherents dispersed. Instead of the long-expected triumph had come the most ignominious defeat, and despair had taken hold of their hearts and minds.

But we should not be too critical of these disciples. Their outlook had been thrown out of focus by the terrible events of Calvary. They were too close to the cross and too concerned with the debris of their shattered hopes to see things clearly. Remember, nearly everyone expected Jesus to take over the Kingdom. Even after the resurrection the disciples put to him the question, "Lord, wilt thou now restore the kingdom?" In a sense everything had pointed toward Jesus' assuming his rightful place as heir to the throne of David. As a direct lineal descendant of David he was in a very real sense a pretender to the throne. That he was so considered is evidenced by the concern of Herod the Great at his birth and the abortive attempt to get rid of him. Perhaps it was for safety's sake that he was known as "Jesus of Nazareth" and not "Jesus of Bethlehem," David's royal city. In any case he had definitely declared his kingship by his fulfillment of the prophecy of Zechariah in the triumphal entry of Palm Sunday, a declaration to which the populace had subscribed their enthusiastic if mistaken approval. Moreover he had actually assumed some measure of regal authority in cleansing the temple.

Of course in Jesus' mind both his kingship and his authority were spiritual, but in the minds of the people it was definitely temporal. Many of his followers had attached themselves to him with that thought in mind. The multitude had been ready when he fed the five thousand to declare him king and to put him on the throne at once. The time seemed ripe.

All of this made the defeat of the cross more terrible. Their high hopes for release from Herod's rule, and perhaps even from Pilate's, had been crushed to pieces by his capture and crucifixion. The whole thing had been tragic. By the first day of the week they could only think of it as a horrible dream which kept revolving in their minds. Their thoughts were still transfixed to a cross which haunted them.

The narratives make it quite clear that they cherished no hopes of a resurrection. The very fact that the Magdalene, Mary, and Salome came bringing spices for his burial is conclusive evidence that they thought of his death as final. Their reluctance to believe is repeatedly recounted. It is true that Jesus had made numerous references to the fact that he would rise again, but evidently in such veiled language that they aroused no real hope and were only recognized after the event. They were all caught in the meshes of the logic of hard facts. The hard realism of the trial and condemnation and the scourging and crucifixion had given a note of finality to his death.

How prone we all are to take the facts for what they appear to be, to accept as conclusive evidence the testimony of the senses! We are so easily and yet often so mistakenly convinced that our world is what we see and know and that its logic is always valid. This is particularly true in our understanding of death.

So the logic of disaster clouded their minds. They had counted on Jesus and on God's vindication of him but all their confidence in him had been betrayed by the course of events. Their hopes were in confusion. Instead of the crown and deliverance there had been only a betrayal and a cross. All their dreams and ideals had been rudely trampled on.

Disappointment and frustrated hopes are always hard to face but in this case their perplexity was increased by the seeming senselessness of it. Their hearts were struggling with the age-old problem: "Right forever on the scaffold; wrong forever on the throne." It was an unlighted tragedy, the Lord of goodness hanging on a criminal's gibbet. They were haunted by his splendor and bewildered by his defeat. You see, the difference between Palm Sunday and Easter was the difference between hope and certainty, but in between lay stark despair.

Then, in the midst of their perplexity as they walked along turning the facts over and over in their minds and trying to find some way to reconcile themselves to life's incongruity but only getting more confused, suddenly a stranger overtook them and fell in by their side, asking if he might join in their conversation which seemed so absorbing. He came just as simply as that. But his first appearances were all gentle and unostentatious: as a gardener to Mary;

as a wayfarer to these heart-weary disciples. But they were not ready for him and did not recognize him. Moreover they found it hard to believe that anyone could have been in Jerusalem during those past three days and be a stranger to the news of the crucifixion. Evidently it had been on every tongue.

Then, they made haste to tell him of the fame and power of Jesus, "Mighty with God and man," and of their own hopes for him. They had hoped that it would have been he who would have redeemed Israel but their hope of a Kingdom had turned to ashes on Golgotha and their hope for a Messiah had been broken on a cross. Three days before, he had been apprehended and crucified and they had been left bereft, nursing their injured sense of justice and their blasted hopes. It is always hard for us to be reconciled to injustice and doubly so if we feel that it lies at the heart of things. The broken hopes that cluster about a fine sense of what should be are the ones that are the hardest to bear. So it was with these disciples.

And then, with a tenderness that was characteristic and yet with a certain authority, he drew their thought from the tragedy of Calvary to the fitness of it. And out of the background of their knowledge of their Scriptures he began to open up a new vision of what the Christ was to be and to do, reminding them of things which they had forgotten or neglected, until the whole experience began to glow with a new light and a deeper meaning, and the sting of the shame of the cross was drawn, and faith and hope began to kindle within them, and the cross and Jesus stood transformed in their eyes.

And he went on to show them that suffering *became* the Messiah, "That it behooved the captain of our salvation to be made perfect through suffering," that it was not only God's will that he face and meet the world's evil and suffer it, but that his very likeness to God demanded it, that the cross was the way of triumph; and the seeming defeat over which they had stumbled became a stepping stone to a deeper understanding of the redemptive Passion of the Christ.

And as they walked and talked their interest mounted and the time passed quickly and before they knew it they were approaching the village. Already the sun was beginning to sink behind the gray hilltops of Ephraim and the lengthening shadows to creep down into the narrow valleys. The laborers had left the plowed fields and the hillside vineyards and were making their way homeward for their evening meal; the bleating sheep were seeking the sheepcot and the travellers were looking for the village inn. Twilight was settling about Emmaus and it would have been folly for the stranger to go further; moreover they felt close to him; and so they constrained him to stay, to come in and sup with them and to warm the fellowship of their table with the light of his faith. Often the rarest gift that we can bestow is not some precious treasure but the courage and confidence that we impart by the strength of our faith.

And so he went in with them and they sat down in the lamplight to the simple evening meal together. It was the natural thing for them to ask him to say grace, and as he took the bread in his hands a miracle of recognition took place. Suddenly he was revealed to them. Perhaps it was the way in which he broke the bread, the old familiar blessing, the turn of his uplifted face; or perhaps in the lamplight they caught a glimpse of the nail prints in his hands— we do not know. But we do know that as he took the bread in those broken hands and brake it they knew him for the Christ. They saw that the answer to their broken hopes, indeed to all broken hopes, was in the revelation of God's love mediated through a cross, and Calvary was turned from a tragedy into a triumph, from a hideous, heart-haunting mistake to a rich, heart-healing revelation of God's power and love.

How much this is like our own experience! So often we too miss him in the way because our perplexity and pre-occupation with our broken hopes and self-concern blind us to his presence, and it is not until we accept the grace of God that we see him, and in him the meaning of suffering and the love behind it. We can only truly see the risen Christ if we see the cross that looms behind him.

That is what makes this incident and the one which follows it the most significant of all the stories of the resurrection. It reveals the very heart of the significance of Easter. The real logic of the resurrection and of the immortality that it brings to light for us lies in the fact that a cross preceded it; that there is power in that cross to make lives ready for a resurrection, fit for a resurrection; that there is testimony in that cross and resurrection that God is able to meet man's sin and the world's evil and suffer it and triumph over it; that He is able to lift us out of the impasse into which we have led life—the death and ruin to which sin and evil lead—and to conquer by sacrifice and love. The trouble is that either we doubt the resurrection entirely or else we accept it for ourselves too easily, too trivially.

The resurrection of man into immortality is not an easy thing that God can do—just like that! He cannot do it easily because it involves a moral universe and sin-ridden men, men who lust and kill and hate and grasp and lie and are proud and cruel and careless and blind and selfish and self-willed. Any look at our world will prove that. Man's resurrection involves judgment and justification on some basis other than just that we are weak and finite and inexperienced and ancestor-ridden. The resurrection is a brilliant triumph but it is not an easy triumph, not just a bit of heavenly legerdemain and surely not just the normal reward for our

being good. For after all, all the goodness we have is from
him. Think of the saints you know of, living or gone, and
try to think how much of their saintliness they would have
if one were to strip all of Christ from their lives and the
lives that have touched them. Aptly enough those who have
the least faith in the cross have the least conviction of the
resurrection. The resurrection demands a cross. Take the
cross and the love and mercy manifest on it away from the
resurrection and all you have left is judgment, hard exacting
judgment. The only resurrection that could be, short of one
which passed through Christ's cross, would be a resurrection
of hard judgment. If in some way God's purposes were not implemented by Christ's cross the resurrection would be either
trivial and morally unreal or it would be terrible and un-
faceable.

The cross and the resurrection stand out like beacon
lights in history not because they shed a roseate light over
life but because they show up things for what they are with
all their evil and misery and cruelty and wilfulness and
declare that God has been able to meet that sin and suffer
it and heal it in Christ, that here in Christ God meets the
destruction that is overtaking us and retrieves life's opportunity, that He meets our folly and cures it, that He
meets our death and through a cross brings life eternal. Any
other view of the resurrection is cheap, superficial sentimentality.

In a world of evil it is inevitable that love should have
to suffer. As one has said, "The crucifixion was the only
kind of thing that could ever happen to God among men."
And what God did was the only kind of thing that a God
of love could do. Love is not afraid of Calvary because it
holds triumph in its hands. Good Friday and Calvary were
not just unhappy occurrences that happened to overtake a
good man. They were the God-intended gateway to Easter.
The way to the empty tomb is via a cross. It was meet that

Christ should have suffered these things to enter into his glory. That is the way to glory always, when love takes up its cross, and out of loyalty to the God we see in Christ, faces and accepts all that evil can do, knowing that love finds its power on a cross.

When these two disciples understood that, then the cross was no longer an offense and they could see and recognize the risen Christ. They realized at last that Good Friday and Easter go together, always. And then what seemed idiotic and utterly futile now became the power of God and the way to triumphant redemption. What seemed utterly unnecessary became for them now the one requisite for man's redemption and the world's hope. For Easter proved forever that the spirit of love in Christ cannot be vanquished or destroyed. It is eternal. And the gift of that love and its triumph is what God offers us through Christ and his resurrection.

And until we accept that cross and share that love and that sacrifice we shall never find the lasting triumph that Easter should bring to us and know the presence of the risen living Christ.

THE EASTER VANGUARD

"He is not here: for he is risen . . . and, behold, he goeth before you into Galilee; there shall ye see him."   Matt. 28:6, 7

IN HIS NOVEL, *Messer Marco Polo,* Donn Byrne tells how the young explorer set out to win the lovely Golden Bells, daughter of Kubla Khan, the mighty Emperor of China, and how before asking for her hand he told to her and to her famous father the story of the Christ. The story he told ran like this:

"High on his throne, so high that his feet were above the heads of his tallest captains, sat the Emperor; and beside him on a little throne sat Golden Bells whose simple charm and beauty were all that the stories of her had foretold. From her throne she smiled at Marco Polo, and, as the Khan smiled also, he began his story, starting with the teachings of the Master, beginning with the Sermon on the Mount.

"One by one he went through the Beatitudes, and everyone listened respectfully; little Golden Bells leaning forward with her chin on her hand, and Kubla Khan leaning backward, his eyes half closed. The young explorer spared no detail, and when he came to the words, 'But I say unto you that ye resist not evil, but whosoever shall smite thee on the right cheek, turn to him the other also,' there was a restless movement among the fighting men in the hall.

"Then he turned from Jesus' teaching to the Master's life and death. He told of Bethlehem and the star and the shepherds, and the poets nodded their heads. He told of the healing deeds and the casting out of devils, and the magicians raised their eyebrows and wondered. He told of the little band in the upper room, of the last supper, and the betrayal of Judas, and the captains of arms shifted in their seats. He told of the judgment, of the scourging, the scarlet robe, and the crown of thorns, and the great Khan flicked his dagger in and out of its sheath, and Golden Bells looked through a mist of tears.

"And then he told of the crucifixion between two thieves, and out from the lips of Kubla Khan there ripped a great oath, and silver tears dropped from the eyes of Golden Bells. Then, in the hush that followed, he added,

'And on the third day he rose again from the dead.' And with a great shout, Kubla Khan stood up and cried, 'He came back from the dead and showed himself to the Roman Pilate in all His majesty and power, he . . .'

" 'No,' said Marco Polo.

" 'Then he showed himself to the thousands who had seen him die on the gallows tree; he showed himself to them; he . . .'

" 'No,' said Marco Polo.

"A frown hovered upon the brow of the Emperor. 'Then to whom did he show himself?'

" 'Just to a few of his friends and followers—a fallen woman named Mary, and to some fisher-folk, and a man named Peter.'

"Kubla Khan sank back and said no more, and silence reigned over that great assembly. And Marco Polo was aware of two things—the great politeness of the Chinese people, and Golden Bell's pitying eyes."

Curious, is it not, but it is true that after the resurrection Jesus did not show himself to Pilate, or to Herod, or even to those who scoffed and railed at him on the cross. He might have gone to the top of the temple pinnacle and declared himself alive again; he could have, but he did not prove his triumph as one normally does.

No, Jesus did not come back to earth again in order to give the glorious lie to cruelty and injustice, or to rip the mask from pride and prejudice and bigotry, to condemn imperious might and high-handed justice, or to show them up for the false and weak things that they are in the universe. He could have done it, if he had not been Jesus Christ. But it would have been of no use. Suppose he had shown himself to Pilate who probably had some misgivings about what he had done? It might very well have paralyzed him with fear or even have driven him mad, and Jesus was not of that spirit. But apart from that, it would only have meant the winning of his case while Jesus was only interested in winning hearts, and hearts are never won through fear. Faith is born of an experience of mercy and providence and love. That is where the power of the cross lies, in the love it reveals. It is possible that Pilate might have believed that Jesus had risen from the dead, but even if he had, that would have been of little value. It is not enough for one to believe that Jesus rose again; one must trust the love that made it possible; one must accept his Lordship and open one's life to his spirit. Belief is not enough; even the devils believe, we are told.

One can see a mighty flash of lightning in the sky and hear its crash and be convinced of its reality and of its power, and yet only be filled with awe and fear of it. It is when that same electrical force is used to light dark streets, or to illuminate homes and warm little children, or to send a song across the ether, that men's hearts are filled with gratitude for it.

Jesus did not show himself to his enemies to force their obeisance nor did he show himself, as one might have expected, to the skeptics to overcome their doubt, or to prove that he was immortal—because he did not return to earth to prove that there was immortality.

Immortality is a very precious and consoling truth but sometimes we are tempted to think of Easter from that viewpoint alone. Of course it does testify that there is that "sweet and blessed country" of which St. Bernard sang. Thank God for that! But Easter and Jesus' resurrection were the inevitable outcome of Jesus' life and spirit. They belonged to heaven, while everybody does not. Moreover being convinced without being converted to his spirit and his way of life means nothing. The resurrection is not primarily to tell us how long life lasts but to reveal to us what lasting life is like.

So Easter was not to convince those who otherwise would never be convinced, even though he did let Thomas put his hands in the nail holes. Jesus made that clear in his comment about the request of Dives in the story of the rich man and Lazarus. You remember Dives, being in torment, wanted someone to be sent back to warn his brothers, which was a laudable request. But Jesus said, "They have Moses and the prophets who have told them how life ought to be lived in order to have an eternal outcome, and if they won't listen to them they will listen to no one even though one might rise from the dead." You see what he was saying is that if they haven't prepared hearts, proof will be useless, and there will be nothing for the proof to take hold of in their minds and hearts. They will still doubt what they want to doubt.

So Jesus did not show himself alive to all men because he could really show himself only to those who would welcome and accept him. It would not mean anything to the others. Ultimately signs and proofs of his resurrection are not of much value. The real significance of it is spiritual, not physical. Only to seeing hearts can he be manifest—only to those who hunger for his spirit, the merciful, the heart-hungry for goodness—for theirs is the Kingdom of which he is the Lord. To them the secret of the resurrection of Christ means something. The resurrection is not for doubters. The resurrection is for loving hearts, for Easter was not intended to convince skeptics but to empower saints.

And so Jesus did not storm and force the citadel of men's hearts with his resurrection appearances. One is to be honored who comes to church to worship on Easter Day and if only for that day, but Easter does not mean the most to those who crowd the church once a year but to those whose hearts are ready for him all the year. So Jesus went back not to the crowds that heard him preach but to those who had given him their loyalty.

We may be slow of heart like the disciples of the road to Emmaus but we can never have the companionship of the resurrected Christ unless we, like them, are disciples of the burning and yearning heart; for Jesus rose to become the Redeemer of those who yearn for his goodness, to become the leader of those who want a living Master to whom to give their lives. Jesus did not suffer and die upon a cross and rise again to prove that he was right. He gave himself on the cross in obedience to the love that was within him, and he rose again to empower that love in the lives of his disciples for the redeeming of the world.

Unhappily we Christians have too often used Easter as a testimony to the past and not as a challenge for the future. He is the risen Christ of our day, not of A.D. 30. The message of the one at the open tomb was, "He is not here. He is risen. Behold he goeth before you!" Behold, he goeth before you! Jesus did not go back to show himself to Pilate and Caiaphas and Herod because he was not going back at all. He was going forward. The triumph of Easter was not so much to vindicate the past as to set free forces of faith for the future. There was no backward look, no reproaches for those who had failed him, no word of blame for Peter's denial: "Ah, Peter, you went back on me there in the courtyard." No word like that! But instead: "Look Peter, out there ahead—my sheep, my lambs. Go feed them!" No word of condemnation for James and John: "You let me down in the Garden. You slept while I agonized." No word like that. But instead: "Go ye into all the world and preach the Gospel of God's love and forgiveness, and lo, I am with you always, even unto the end of the world." No turning back to the past but rather pointing men's hearts and minds toward the future, leaving the past behind, forgiven.

There is a word here for us today. We are living in a day of change and uncertainty. Who knows what the future will bring? But of this we may be sure. We can go on with courage and confidence because the love of God belongs to the future. We may not know what is before us, but we do know Who is before us. We may not know what is out there ahead, but we do know that Christ is out there ahead and that nothing can separate us from the love of Christ, neither things present nor things to come. Calvary could not stop him. The grave could not hold him. They nailed him to a cross and shut him up in a cave behind a great stone and put a seal upon it and guards beside it to keep him in but the next thing we know, "He is out ahead," and the next word we have is, "He is not dead. He is risen. Behold he goeth before you."

That is the real heart of the Easter message: the reality of the living, ongoing Christ, the pioneer of God, leading us on in every project for good, every enterprise of God that will bring the love of God into contact with the lives of men.

"Behold, he goeth before you." Where? Where would you expect to find the Christ in a world that is still suffering from evil and sin? On a throne? A spectator to the scene, or down in the midst of things, by the side of those who share his spirit and are working to bring about a better world, to bring peace and understanding and justice and help to those in need, making the love of God reasonable and real through the living Christ's power!

That is the real heart of the Easter message. The point is not whether Jesus proved men's immortality but whether he himself lives and leads and challenges our life today, whether he impinges on life not as a memory or a historic figure of the first century but as a contemporary companion and a living leader, a guiding spirit and an eternal harbinger of heavenly hope on earth.

That is what counts and that is what is unique about the resurrection. It brought a triumphant Christ into eternal contact with our world, challenging our careless capitulation to evil, arresting our complacent self-centeredness, restraining our selfishness, awakening our trust in God, illuminating our hearts with the grace of his spirit, and guiding our reluctant spirits into ways of good will and good enterprise. Easter assures us daily that the love and concern of God knows no limits and desireth only our good. That is why Easter is unique and revolutionary.

It guarantees to us who are beset by evil and confronted with difficulty the eternal love and power of God to redeem our lives and renew our spirits, for it makes the love that went to a cross accessible to us every day through the companionship and guidance of the living triumphant Christ.

> For warm, sweet, tender, even yet a present help is He,
>   And faith has still its Olivet and love its Galilee.
> The healing of His seamless dress is by our beds of pain.
>   We touch Him in life's throng and press and we are whole again.

"Lo, I am with thee always, even unto the end of the world."